10 Minute Guide to PowerPoint®

Joe Kraynak and Seta Frantz

alpha
books

A Division of Prentice Hall Computer Publishing

11711 North College, Carmel, Indiana 46032 USA

To my brother Randy, a very funny guy.
To Scott with all my love.

© **1993 by Alpha Books**

International Standard Book Number: 1-56761-135-4
Library of Congress Catalog Card Number: 92-75156

95 94 93   8 7 6 5 4 3

Interpretation of the printing code: the rightmost number of the first series of numbers is the year of the book's printing; the rightmost number of the second series of numbers is the number of the book's printing. For example, a printing code of 93-1 shows that the first printing of the book occurred in 1993.

Publisher: *Marie Butler-Knight*
Associate Publisher: *Lisa A. Bucki*
Managing Editor: *Elizabeth Keaffaber*
Manuscript Editor: *Barry Childs-Helton*
Interior Design: *Amy Peppler-Adams*
Cover Design: *Dan Armstrong*
Indexer: *Jeanne Clark*
Production: *Tim Cox, Mark Enochs, Tim Groeling, Phil Kitchel, Bob LaRoche, Tom Loveman, Angela M. Pozdol, Carrie Roth, Susan Shepard, Kelli Widdifield*

Special thanks to Michael Hanks for ensuring the technical accuracy of this book.

Screen reproductions in this book were created by means of the program Collage Plus from Inner Media Inc., Hollis, NH.

Printed in the United States of America

Contents

Trademarks

All terms mentioned in this book that are known to be trademarks or service marks are listed below. In addition, terms suspected of being trademarks or service marks have been appropriately capitalized. Alpha Books cannot attest to the accuracy of this information. Use of a term in this book should not be regarded as affecting the validity of any trademark or service mark.

Microsoft and PowerPoint are registered trademarks, and Toolbox, TrueType, and Windows are trademarks of Microsoft Corporation.

Introduction

You may have heard that PowerPoint is powerful and easy to use—that it allows you to quickly create and modify slide and overhead presentations and create printouts of your presentations. But now that you have the program, where do you start?

A few things are certain:

- You need to learn the program quickly.

- You need to identify and learn only the information necessary to perform a specific task.

- You need some clear-cut, plain-English instructions that tell you what to do.

Welcome to the *10 Minute Guide to PowerPoint*.

What Is a 10 Minute Guide?

The 10 Minute Guide series is a new approach to learning computer programs. Like all 10 Minute Guides, this one is divided into a series of over 20 lessons, each designed to be completed in 10 minutes or less. Each lesson is a self-contained series of steps that teaches you how to perform a specific task.

What is PowerPoint?

PowerPoint is a *presentation graphics program*. That is, it allows you to place text, art, and graphs on *slides* to create a slide show. The slide show can then be printed, displayed on-screen, or transformed into 35mm slides or overhead transparencies. A sample slide is shown in Figure I.1.

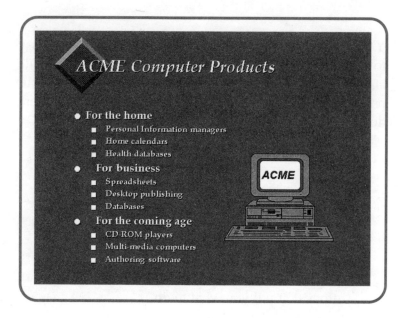

Figure I.1   A sample slide created with PowerPoint.

Understanding Presentations

A *presentation* is a collection of slides designed to present an idea, prove a point, or convince an audience to take some action. With PowerPoint you can create the slides you want to include in the presentation in any order. PowerPoint provides the tools you need to rearrange the slides later.

Speaker Notes and Audience Handouts

In addition to creating slides, you can use PowerPoint to create speaker notes pages and audience handouts. Each speaker notes page can include a copy of one of the slides in the presentation plus any details the speaker wants to point out.

Audience handouts contain copies of all the slides including any text that the presenter wants to add. Handouts provide the audience with a way of reviewing the material later.

Conventions Used in This Book

Each mini-lesson in this book is set up in an easily accessible format. Steps that you must perform are numbered. Pictures of screens show you what to expect. And the following icons point out definitions, warnings, and tips to help you understand what you're doing and avoid trouble:

Plain English icons appear wherever a new term is defined.

Panic Button icons appear where new users commonly run into trouble.

Timesaver Tips offer shortcuts and hints for using the program effectively.

In addition, the following conventions are used to provide a clear idea of what to do:

`What you type`	The information we want you to type appears in color.
Keys you press or items you select	If you are told to press a key or select an item, the key or item appears in second color. If the item has an underlined selection letter, that letter appears in bold color.
`On-screen text`	Any text that appears on-screen is printed in a special monospace font.
Menu names	Whenever we mention the name of a menu or screen, the first letter of its name is capitalized.

How to Use This Book

If you are new to Microsoft Windows, work through the Windows primer at the back of this book. This primer leads you through the Windows basics, explaining how to use the mouse and how to enter commands in Windows.

If you haven't yet installed PowerPoint, turn to the inside front cover of this book for installation instructions.

Once you know the Windows basics and have installed PowerPoint, you can work through this book from Lesson 1 to the end, or skip to any lesson in the book, as needed.

Lesson 1

Starting and Exiting PowerPoint

In this lesson, you will learn how to start and exit PowerPoint, and you will learn about the parts of the PowerPoint presentation screen.

Starting PowerPoint

Before you start PowerPoint, you should have a basic understanding of how to get around in Microsoft Windows. If you need a refresher course in Windows, read the Windows Primer at the back of this book. To start PowerPoint, perform the following steps:

1. Start Windows and display the Program Manager.

2. If the Microsoft PowerPoint program group is not displayed, click on Window in the menu bar and select Microsoft PowerPoint.

3. Double-click on the Microsoft PowerPoint icon, or use the arrow keys to highlight the icon, and press Enter. PowerPoint starts, and a blank Presentation window appears (see Figure 1.1).

1

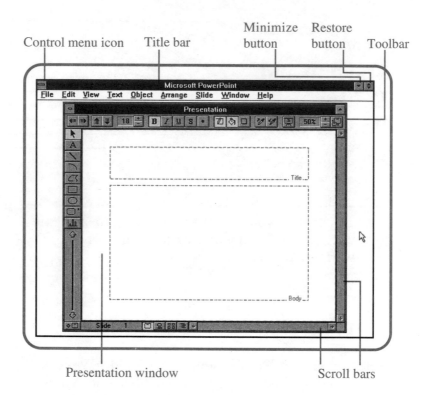

Figure 1.1 The Microsoft PowerPoint application window.

A Look at PowerPoint's Application Window

The PowerPoint window (shown in Figure 1.1) contains the same elements you will find in most Windows programs: a Control menu icon, a title bar, Minimize and Restore buttons, and so on. For an explanation of these elements, refer to the Windows Primer at the back of this book.

In the center of the PowerPoint window is a *Presentation window*. You will use this window to create your slides and arrange the slides in a presentation. This window contains a Tool Palette, a Toolbar, and additional tools, which are described in the following sections.

The Tool Palette

The Tool Palette contains the following tools that allow you to add objects, captions, and graphs to your slides:

 Selection tool   If you select this tool, the mouse pointer turns into an arrow. You can then use the pointer to select, move, and resize objects on a slide.

What's an Object?   An *object* is any item that you place on a slide. An object can be a text box, a graph, a simple line, or a complex illustration.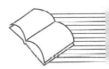

 Text tool   Allows you to add labels, captions, or paragraphs to a slide.

 Line tool   Lets you draw a straight line using your mouse.

 Arc tool   Allows you to draw a curve using your mouse.

Freeform tool   Lets you draw an irregular shape using your mouse.

Rectangle tool   Lets you draw a rectangle with square corners.

 Ellipse tool   Lets you use the mouse to draw a circle or oval.

 Shape tool   When you select this tool (by clicking and holding the left mouse button), a menu of shapes appears. You can select the shape you want to draw, and then use your mouse to draw it.

 Graph tool   Lets you create or import a graph into a slide.

To select a tool in the Presentation window, move the mouse pointer over the tool and click the left mouse button.

The Toolbar

The Toolbar, located just below the Presentation window title bar, places the following commonly used commands and formatting tools at your fingertips:

 **Outline buttons**   If you are creating an outline, use these buttons to move a paragraph in the outline left or right to change its level in the outline and up or down to change its place in the outline.

Text Formatting buttons   Use these buttons to change the size of the text; to make the text bold, italic, or underlined; to add a shadow to the text; or to add a bullet symbol.

Object Attribute buttons   These buttons allow you to change the appearance of a graphic object. You can draw a line (border) around the object, fill the object with a color, or add a shadow to the object.

Apply Style buttons   These buttons allow you to pick up styles from existing text or objects and apply the styles to other text or objects.

What's a Style?   A style is a collection of formats applied to an object. For example, if you use 24-point bold, italic text, the style consists of three formats: 24-point, bold, and italic.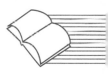

Slide Show button   This button displays an on-screen slide show using the slides you created. This allows you to preview the slide you create.

Scale buttons   These buttons allow you to zoom in on a slide to see more detail, or zoom out to see the entire slide. The Home View button switches back and forth between the fit-in-window size and the previous view you chose.

The Slide Buttons

In addition to the buttons in the Toolbar and the Tool Palette, PowerPoint provides several tools for working with the slides in a presentation. These tools are located in the lower left corner of the Presentation window:

 **Slide Changer**   The Slide Changer allows you to change from one slide to the next. Drag the lever on the Slide Changer down to display the next slide, or up to display the previous slide.

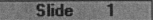 **Slide Counter**   As you move from one slide to the next in a presentation, the slide counter displays the number of the currently displayed slide.

 New Slide button   The New Slide button creates a new, blank slide in the presentation.

 **View buttons**   The View buttons switch the display to show different elements of the presentation. Initially, the Slide View button is pressed so only one slide appears on-screen at a time. In Note view, you can see the notes added to each slide. Slide Sorter view allows you to rearrange the slides by moving small versions of the slides on-screen. Outline view allows you to create and work with a presentation as an outline.

Getting Help

If you need help performing a task in PowerPoint, you can use PowerPoint's on-line help. To get help, pull down the Help menu and select Contents or press F1. A list of Help topics appears, as shown in Figure 1.2.

Context-sensitive Help If a dialog box is displayed on-screen, you can view information about that dialog box by pressing the F1 key.

Click on a topic to select it.

Figure 1.2 The Help table of contents displays a list of topics

Navigating the Help System

To view information about one of the topics listed, click on the topic or tab to it and press Enter. Another Help window will appear, with information about the selected topic. This window may also contain two types of *hypertext links* (solid- and dotted-underlined) that let you get more information about related topics.

7

If you select a topic that is solid-underlined, PowerPoint will open a Help window for that topic. If you select a term that is dotted-underlined, PowerPoint displays a definition for that term. To select a topic or term, click on it or tab to it and press Enter.

Using the Help Buttons

At the top of the Help window is the following series of buttons, designed to help you move around the Help system. To use one of the buttons, click on it, or press the key that corresponds to the highlighted letter in the button's name.

Contents   Displays a list of Help topics from which you can choose.

Search   Lets you search for a Help topic by typing the topic's name or part of its name.

Back   Takes you back to the previous Help window.

History   Displays a list of Help topics you most recently looked at.

<<   Goes back to a previous Help screen in a related series of Help screens.

>>   Displays the next Help screen in a related series of Help screens.

Exiting PowerPoint

To leave PowerPoint, perform any of the following steps:

- Open the File menu and select Exit.

- Press Alt+F4.

- Double-click on PowerPoint's Control menu icon.

In this lesson, you learned how to start and exit PowerPoint, you learned about the parts of the Presentation window, and you learned how to get on-line help. In the next lesson, you will learn how to create and save a presentation.

Preparing for a Presentation

In this lesson, you will learn how to prepare for a new presentation by selecting a printer and choosing a slide setup.

Choosing a Target Printer

Before you start creating slides, speaker's notes, and audience handouts, you should select the printer(s) you want to use. By selecting a printer, you are telling PowerPoint which typestyles and type sizes are available on that printer, and for your presentations.

If you have only one printer, and you already use it for all your Windows applications, you do not have to select a printer (just use the printer you set up in Windows). However, if you use two printers (say, a color printer and a black-and-white printer), you should specify which printer you want to use for slides (usually a color printer), and which one for speaker's notes and audience handouts (usually a black-and-white printer). To select a printer, perform the following steps:

1. Open the File menu and select Print Setup. The Print Setup dialog box appears, as shown in Figure 2.1.

10

2. In the Slides option group, select the printer you want to use for printing your slides. Either choose Default Printer (to choose the currently active Windows printer), or choose Specific Printer and select a printer from the drop-down list.

3. To enter any specific details about the selected printer, click on the Setup button to the right of the Slides option group, and enter the desired information. (For more information about setting up a printer in Windows, refer to your Windows documentation.)

4. In the Notes, Handouts and Outline option group, select the printer you want to use for printing speaker's notes, audience handouts, and outlines. Either choose Default Printer, or choose Specific Printer and select a printer from the drop-down list.

5. To enter any specific details about the selected printer, click on the Setup button to the right of the Slides option group, and enter the desired information.

6. Click on the OK button, or tab to it and press Enter.

Figure 2.1 Use the Print Setup dialog box to select the printer(s) you want to use.

Changing Printers Later   If you select a different printer later, the new printer may not offer fonts
that match the fonts of the original printer.
PowerPoint will attempt to find the closest available font, but you should still go back through the
slides and make sure the font substitutions are to
your liking.

Choosing a Slide Setup

A *slide setup* tells PowerPoint the dimensions of the paper,
slides, or transparencies on which to print. By specifying
the dimensions before you start creating your slides, you
will have a more accurate picture of how the slides will look
as you are creating them. To choose a slide setup, perform
the following steps:

1. Open the File menu and select Slide Setup . The Slide
    Setup dialog box appears, as shown in Figure 2.2.

2. Open the Slides Sized for drop-down list, and select one
    of the following options:

    On-screen Show   This option sets the width and height
    of the slides specifically for an electronic presentation.

    Letter Paper (8.5 x 11 in)   This is the default setting. It
    prints the slides sideways on 8.5-by-11-inch paper.

    A4 Paper (210 x 297 mm)   Select this option to print
    on international-size paper.

    35mm Slides   This option creates slides that can
    be transformed into actual 35mm slides for a slide

projector. You can send your presentation file to an outside vendor to have it transformed into slides.

Custom   Select this option to specify dimensions that are not listed. Use the Width and Height boxes below the drop-down list to enter the dimensions in inches.

3. Select one of the following options in the Orientation group to specify the direction you want the slides printed:

Portrait   This option prints the slide as you would print a business letter—the slide is taller than it is wide.

Landscape   This option prints the slide along the wide edge of the page, making the slide wider than it is tall.

4. To start numbering the slides with a number other than 1, enter a number in the Number Slides From box. (You may want to start with a different number, for example, if this presentation picks up where another left off.)

5. Click on the OK button. A warning box may appear, telling you that you may have to edit all existing slides if you changed the dimensions.

6. Because you have no existing slides, click on the Change button. This puts the dimension changes into effect.

Existing Slides   If you change the dimensions after creating one or more slides, PowerPoint automatically scales the slides according to the new dimensions. You should review the slides to make sure they still look the way you want them to look.

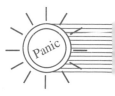

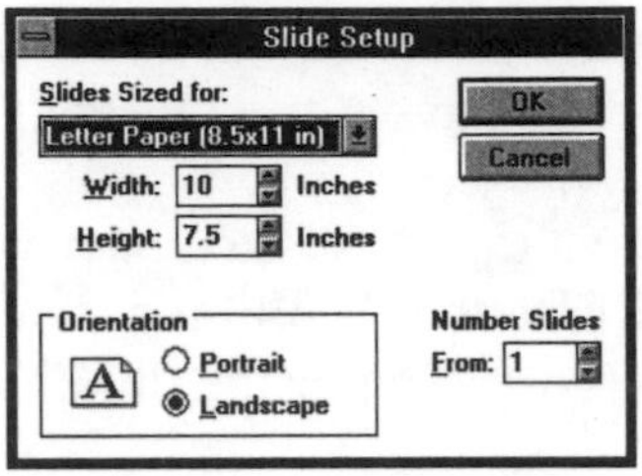

Figure 2.2 Use the Slide Setup dialog box to specify the dimensions, orientation, and numbering of the slides.

In this lesson, you learned how to choose a printer and a slide setup to tell PowerPoint how you intend to reproduce your slides, notes, and audience handouts. In the next lesson, you will learn how to save, close, and open a presentation.

Saving, Closing, and Opening Presentations

In this lesson, you will learn how to save a presentation to disk, close a presentation, and open a new or existing presentation.

Saving a Presentation

Although you have not yet created a slide, it is a good idea to save your presentation and give it a name. Once you have saved the file for the first time, you can quickly save any additional work you do on the presentation later.

To save a presentation for the first time, perform the following steps:

1. Open the File menu and select Save , or press Ctrl+S . The Save As dialog box appears, as shown in Figure 3.1.

2. In the File Name text box, type the name you want to assign to the presentation (up to eight characters). (Do not type a filename extension; PowerPoint will automatically add the extension .PPT.)

3. To save the file to a different disk drive, pull down the Drives drop-down list and select the letter of the drive.

4. To save the file in a different directory, select the directory from the Directory list.

5. Click on the OK button. The file is saved to disk.

Quick Saves Now that you have named the file and saved it to disk, you can save any changes you make to the presentation simply by pressing Ctrl+S.

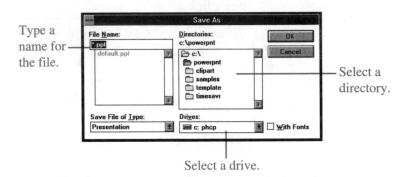

Type a name for the file.

Select a directory.

Select a drive.

Figure 3.1 The Save As dialog box.

To create a copy of a presentation under a different name, open the File menu and select the Save As command. Use the Save As dialog box to enter a different name for the copy. You can then modify the copy without affecting the original.

Closing a Presentation

You can close a presentation at any time. This closes the Presentation window, and allows you to use the space on-screen for a different presentation. To close a presentation, perform the following steps:

1. If more than one Presentation window is displayed, click on any portion of the window you want to close. This activates the window.

2. Open the File menu and select Close, or press Ctrl+F4. If you have not saved the presentation, or if you haven't saved your most recent changes, a dialog box appears, as shown in Figure 3.2, asking if you want to save your changes.

3. To save your changes, click on the Yes button. If this is a new presentation, the Save As dialog box appears, as in Figure 3.1. If you have saved the file previously, your changes are saved in the file, and the Presentation window closes.

4. If the Save As dialog box appears, enter a name for the file and any other information as explained earlier. Then, click on the OK button.

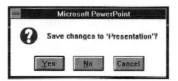

Figure 3.2 If you try to close a presentation without saving your work, PowerPoint warns you.

Opening a Presentation

You can open a new or previously created presentation at any time, and you can have more than one presentation displayed on-screen. The following sections explain how to open a new or existing presentation.

17

Opening a New Presentation

Whenever you want to start creating a new presentation from scratch, you can open a new Presentation window. To open a new presentation, perform the following steps:

1. Open the File menu and select New. If no presentation is currently open, a new Presentation window appears. If a presentation is open, PowerPoint displays the New dialog box, shown in Figure 3.3.

2. Choose one of the following options to specify the format you want to use for the new presentation:

   Use format of active presentation   Choose this option if you want to use the format of an existing presentation that is currently displayed on-screen.

   Use default format   Choose this option if you want to use PowerPoint's default format.

3. Click on the OK button. PowerPoint opens a new Presentation window.

Opening an Existing Presentation

Once you have saved a presentation to disk, you can open the presentation and continue working on it at any time. You can also open a sample PowerPoint presentation to get some ideas for your own presentation or to use the format from the presentation. To open an existing presentation, perform the following steps:

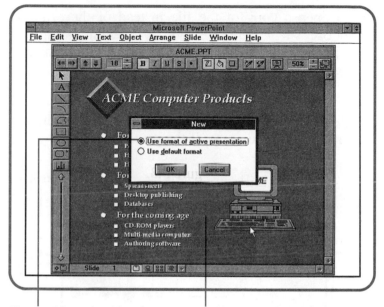

Choose this option if you want to use the
same format as the active presentation.

Figure 3.3 The New dialog box asks you to specify
the format you want to use for the presentation.

1. Open the File menu and select Open, or press Ctrl+O.
   The Open dialog box appears.

2. Pull down the Drives drop-down list, and select the
   letter of the drive on which the file is stored.

3. In the Directories list, select the directory in which the
   presentation file is stored. The list below the File Name
   text box displays the names of all the presentation files
   (files that end in .PPT) in the selected directory.

4. In the list below the File Name text box, click on the
   file you think you want to open. The first slide in the
   presentation appears in the preview area (see Figure 3.4).

19

5. To open a copy of the file instead of the original, choose Open Untitled Copy. By opening an untitled copy, you can change the presentation without affecting the original.

6. To open the presentation file, double-click on its filename, or highlight the filename and click on the OK button. PowerPoint opens the presentation.

The first slide in the selected presentation

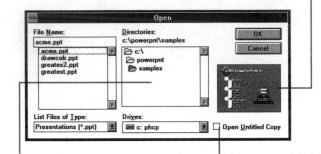

Current directory   Click here to open an untitled copy.

Figure 3.4   The Open dialog box lets you select and preview the presentation.

View a Sample Presentation   PowerPoint comes with several sample presentations, which are stored in the \POWERPT\SAMPLES directory. To get a general idea of how a slide show works, open one of these samples, and use the slide changer to flip through the slides. Or open a sample as an untitled copy, and modify it to suit your needs.

In this lesson, you learned how to save, close, and open presentations. In the next lesson, you will learn how to apply a template to your presentation to give your slides a professional and consistent look.

Lesson 4
Using PowerPoint's Templates and Slide Master

In this lesson, you will learn how to give your presentation a professional and consistent look by using PowerPoint's templates.

Understanding Templates and Slide Masters

PowerPoint comes with over 160 professionally designed slides you can use as *templates* for your own presentations. That is, you can apply one of these predesigned slides to your own presentation, to give the slides in your presentation the same look as the professional slides.

What Is a Template?   A template is a predesigned slide that comes with PowerPoint. It contains a color scheme and a general layout for each slide in the presentation. The template makes it easy for you to create a presentation; you simply fill in the blanks on each slide.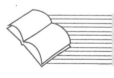

Each template has a *Slide Master* that works in the background to control the background color, layout, and style of each slide in the presentation. This provides all the slides in your presentation with a consistent look. In the following sections, you will learn how to select a template for your presentation and modify the Slide Master.

Selecting a Template

Any PowerPoint presentation file can act as a template. Initially, you will want to use one of PowerPoint's sample files as a template for your presentation. However, once you have created a presentation of your own, you can use it as a template, as well. To apply a template to your presentation, perform the following steps:

1. Open the File menu and select Apply Template. The Apply Template dialog box appears.

2. In the Directories list, change to the C:\POWERPNT \TEMPLATE directory. The template subdirectories appear. Each subdirectory contains a set of templates for a particular type of presentation: 35mm slides, black-and-white overheads, color overheads, and on-screen video presentations.

3. Select the template subdirectory for the type of presentation you want to create. A list of templates appears in the File Name list.

4. Click on a file name in the list, or tab to the list and use the ↓ key to highlight a name. When you highlight the name of a template, a slide appears in the preview area, showing what the template looks like. (See Figure 4.1.)

5. Press Enter or double-click on the name of the template you want to use. You are returned to your presentation, and the template is now in control of your presentation.

Template directory   35mslide directory

Apply Template

File Name:
vividln3.ppt
award3.ppt
banner3.ppt
bevel3.ppt
blackbx3.ppt
blstrip3.ppt
bludiag3.ppt
bluebox3.ppt
bluegrn3.ppt
blugray3.ppt

Directories:
c:\...\template\35mslide
c:\
powerpnt
template
35mslide

OK
Cancel

List Files of Type:
Presentations [*.ppt]

Drives:
c: phcp

A list of templates in
the current directory

Preview of template

Figure 4.1   The Apply Template dialog box lets you preview a template before you apply it.

Apply Templates at Any Time.   You do not have to apply a template before you begin creating your presentation. You can change the template at any time, and your entire presentation will take on the look of the new template. Note that a template will replace any background infromation you have added in Slide Master with its own. For more information on background information, see Lesson 16.

Editing the Slide Master

Every presentation has a Slide Master that controls the overall appearance and layout of each slide. A sample Slide Master is shown in Figure 4.2.

All slide titles will appear in this style.

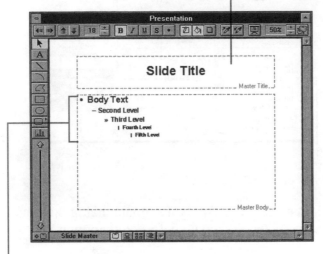

The master body text on each slide will appear in this style.

Figure 4.2   The Slide Master ensures that all slides in a presentation have a consistent look.

The two most important elements on the Slide Master are the *Master Title* and *Master Body* objects. The Master Title object contains the formatting specifications for each slide's title; that is, it tells PowerPoint the type size, style, and color to use for the text in the title of each slide. The Master Body object contains the formatting specifications for all remaining text on the slide. For most of PowerPoint's templates, the Master Body object sets up specifications for a bulleted list: these include the type of bullet, as well as the type styles, sizes, and indents for each item in the list.

In addition to the Master Title and Body, the Slide Master can contain the background color, a border, a code that inserts page numbers, your company logo, a clip art object, and any other elements you want to appear on *every* slide in the presentation.

To view the Slide Master for a presentation, perform the following steps:

1. Open the View menu and select Slide Master. The Slide Master appears, as shown in Figure 4.2.

2. To return to Slide view, open the View menu and select Slides, or click on the Slide view button as shown here:

Missing the View? To return to Slide view, you must have a slide or an active presentation on-screen.

The Slide Master is like any slide. In the following lessons, when you learn how to add text, graphics, borders, and other objects to a slide, keep in mind that you can add these objects on individual slides or on the Slide Master. When you add the objects to the Slide Master, the objects will appear on *every* slide in the presentation.

In this lesson, you learned how to give your presentation a consistent look by applying a template to it. You also learned how to display the Slide Master. In the next lesson, you will learn how to create a basic slide.

Lesson 5
Creating a Slide

In this lesson, you will learn how to create a basic slide, add a slide to a presentation, and move from slide to slide.

Creating Your First Slide

In the previous lesson, you learned that the Slide Master contains two objects: a Master Title and a Master Body. When you switch to Slide view, you will see a slide that contains two similar objects: the *Title object* and the *Body object* (see Figure 5.1). In the following sections, you will learn how to type text into these objects to create a slide.

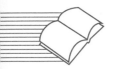 **The Slide Master Is in Control** When typing a title and bulleted list, keep in mind that the Slide Master is controlling the appearance of the title and bulleted list on each slide.

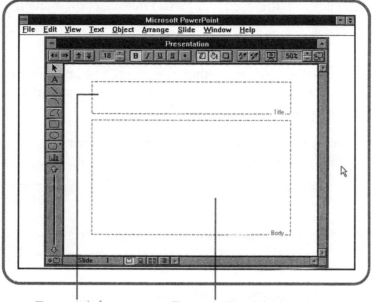

Type a title here.   Type a bulleted list here.

Figure 5.1   You can create a slide by typing a title and a bulleted list.

Creating a Slide in Slide View

In Slide view, one slide is displayed on-screen at a time. You can type text for the existing objects (Title and Body) and add objects on this slide to create the look you want. To add a title and bulleted list in Slide view, perform the following steps:

1. Type a title in the Title object. When you start typing, the Title object gets smaller to show the actual size of the text, and the insertion point appears:

ACME Computer Products

2. Click on the Body object. The selection rectangle appears around the Body object, showing the object is active.

3. Type the first entry that you want to appear in the bulleted list. As you type, the Body object gets smaller, and a bullet appears to the left of your text.

4. Press Enter. Another bullet appears, showing that you can type another entry for the list.

5. Continue typing entries until you have completed the list.

Too Looong   If your text is too long for the slide, consider continuing onto another slide, creating two columns, or changing the font and size of the text (see Lesson 8).

Creating a Slide in Outline View

In Slide view, slides are not displayed as actual slides. Instead, PowerPoint displays the title and bulleted list that appears on each slide. In other words, the presentation appears as an outline. To create a slide in Outline view, perform the following steps:

1. Open the View menu and select Outline, or click on the Outline button as shown:

This changes to Outline view.

2. Type a title for the first slide you want to create.

3. Press Enter. PowerPoint starts a new line of text, keeping the new line at the same outline level as the previous line—the title level.

4. Click on the Demote button to indent the line one level, or press Alt+Shift+→. PowerPoint indents the line and displays a bullet.

5. Type the first entry that you want to appear in the bulleted list.

6. Press Enter. Another bullet appears, showing that you can type another entry for the list. (See Figure 5.2.)

7. Continue typing entries until you have completed the list.

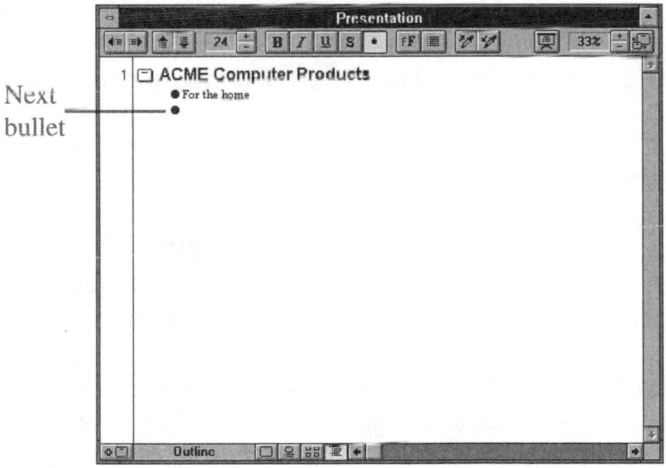

Figure 5.2 Each time you press Enter, a bullet appears, allowing you to type an entry.

Not Every Slide Needs a Title and Bulleted List The title and bulleted list are convenient for creating a presentation. However, they are not essential. If you want to create a slide that does not contain a title or bulleted list, select the Title text or Body text box and press Del. You can then add any other objects you want to the slide as explained in later lessons.

Working with a Bulleted List

The bulleted list is a powerful tool for helping you organize and present ideas and supporting data for your presentation. As you type entries, keep in mind that you can change an entry's level and position in the list. To change the position or level of an entry, use the arrow keys or mouse to move the insertion point anywhere inside the entry, and then perform one of the following actions:

Click on this button to move the entry up in the list.

Click on this button to move the entry down in the list.

 Click on this button to indent the entry to the next lower level in the list. The item will be indented, the bullet will change, and the text will usually appear smaller.

 Click on this button to remove the indent and move the entry to the next higher level in the list. The item will be moved to the left, the bullet will change, and the text will appear larger.

Dragging Paragraphs   You can quickly change the position or level of a paragraph by dragging it up, down, left, or right. To drag a paragraph, move the mouse pointer to the left side of the paragraph until it turns into a four-headed arrow. Then, hold down the mouse button and drag the paragraph to the desired position.

In later lessons, you will learn how to change the appearance of the bullet, the style and size of text for each entry, and the amount the text is indented for each level.

Adding a Slide to Your Presentation

When you are finished creating your first slide, you may want to add another slide to your presentation. To add a slide, perform any of the following steps:

- Click on the New Slide button, as shown:

- Press Ctrl+N.

- Open the Slide menu and select New Slide.

- In Outline view, press Enter after the last bulleted item, and then click on the Promote button, as shown below, or press Alt+Shift+← until you are at the Title level in the outline:

Moving from Slide to Slide

When you have more than one slide in your presentation, you will need to move from one slide to the next in order to work with a specific slide. The procedure for moving to a slide depends on whether you are working in Slide view or Outline view:

- In Outline view, use your mouse or the cursor-movement keys to move to the slide you want to work with.

- In Slide view, drag the Slide Changer (see Figure 5.3) until the slide you want to work with is displayed. Then release the mouse button.

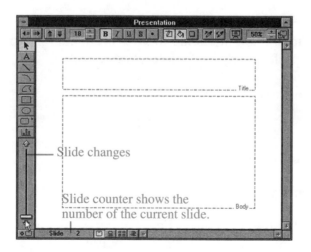

Figure 5.3 Drag the Slide Changer to change to the next slide.

In this lesson, you learned how to create a basic slide, add a slide to your presentation, and move from slide to slide. In the next lesson, you will learn how to create additional text objects.

Lesson 6

Adding a Text Object to a Slide

In this lesson, you will learn how to add a label and text box to a slide and how to align the text.

Adding a Label to a Slide

Labels are small amounts of text that allow you to call attention to important elements on the slide. For example, if you are creating a training presentation, labels might point to important parts of a machine. To add a label to a slide, perform the following steps:

1. Click on the Text tool as shown here:

2. Move the mouse pointer to where you want the label to start (anywhere off the Title and Body objects), and click the left mouse button. A blinking *insertion point* appears, showing where the text will be inserted.

3. Type the label.

4. Click anywhere outside the label.

If you go back and click on the label, a *selection box* will appear around the label, as shown in Figure 6.1. You can drag the box to move it, or drag a corner of the box (as shown) to resize it. PowerPoint will wrap the text automatically, as needed to fit inside the box.

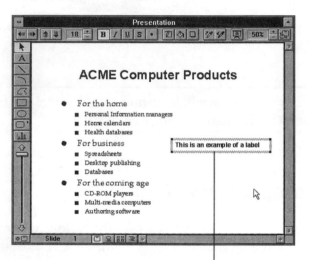

Label surrounded by a selection box

Figure 6.1   Click on your label after creating it to display the selection box.

Adding a Text Box to a Slide

A *text box* is similar to a label, but is generally used for holding more text (for example, an entire paragraph or a bulleted list). To create a text box, perform the following steps:

1. Click on the Text tool as shown here:

2. Move the mouse pointer to where you want the upper left corner of the text box to appear (anywhere off the Title and Body objects).

3. Hold down the mouse button, and drag the mouse pointer to the right until the box is the desired width.

4. Release the mouse button. A one-line text box appears. (See Figure 6.2.)

5. Type the text that you want to appear in the text box. When you reach the right side of the box, PowerPoint wraps the text to the next line, and makes the box one line longer. To start a new paragraph, press Enter.

6. Click anywhere outside the text box.

If you click on the text box, a selection box will appear, as shown in Figure 6.1. You can drag the box to move it or drag a corner of the box to resize it. PowerPoint will wrap the text automatically, as needed to fit inside the box.

Figure 6.2   A one-line text box appears.

Editing Text in a Text Object

To edit text in a text object, first click on the text object to select it, and click on the Text tool. Then, perform any of the following steps:

- *To select text,* drag the I-beam pointer (see Figure 6.3) over the text you want to select. (To select a single word, double-click on it.)

35

- *To delete text,* select the text and press the Del key.

- *To insert text,* click the mouse pointer where you want the text inserted, and then type the text.

- *To replace text,* select the text you want to replace, and then type the new text. When you start typing, the selected text is deleted.

- *To copy and paste text,* select the text you want to copy, and choose the Copy command from the Edit menu, or press Ctrl+C. Move the insertion point to where you want the text pasted (it can be in a different text box), and choose Paste from the Edit menu, or press Ctrl+V.

- *To cut and paste (move) text,* select the text you want to cut, and choose the Cut command from the Edit menu, or press Ctrl+X. Move the insertion point to where you want the text pasted (it can be in a different text box), and choose Paste from the Edit menu, or press Ctrl+V.

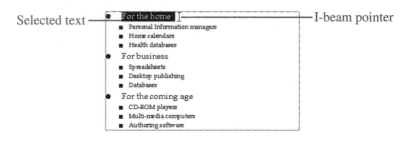

Figure 6.3   To select text, drag the I-beam pointer over the text.

Changing the Text Alignment and Line Spacing

When you first type text, it is set against the left edge of the text box and is single-spaced. In this section, you will learn how to change a paragraph's alignment and line spacing.

You can change the alignment for any paragraph in a text box by performing the following steps:

1. Click anywhere inside the paragraph whose alignment you want to change.

2. Open the Text menu and select Alignment. The Alignment submenu appears.

3. Select Left, Center, Right, or Justify, to align the paragraph as desired. (See Figure 6.4 for examples.)

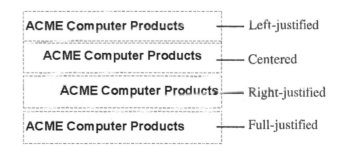

Figure 6.4   You can align each paragraph in a text box.

Quick Key Alignment   To quickly set the alignment for a paragraph, click inside the paragraph and press one of the following key combinations: Ctrl+[for left alignment, Ctrl+] for right alignment, or Ctrl+\ to center the text.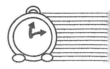

To change the line spacing in a paragraph, perform these steps:

1. Click inside the paragraph whose line spacing you want to change, or select all the paragraphs whose line spacing you want to change.

2. Open the Text menu and select Line Spacing. The Line Spacing dialog box appears, as shown in Figure 6.5.

3. Click on the arrow buttons to the right of any of the following text boxes to change the line spacing:

   Line Spacing   This setting controls the space between the lines in a paragraph.

   Before Paragraph   This setting controls the space between this paragraph and the paragraph that comes before it.

   After Paragraph   This setting controls the space between this paragraph and the paragraph that comes after it.

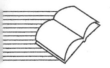

Lines or Points?   The drop-down list box that appears to the right of each setting allows you to set the line spacing in *lines* or *points*. A line is the current line height. A point is a unit commonly used to measure text. A point is approximately 1/72 of an inch.

4. Click on the OK button. Your line spacing changes are put into effect.

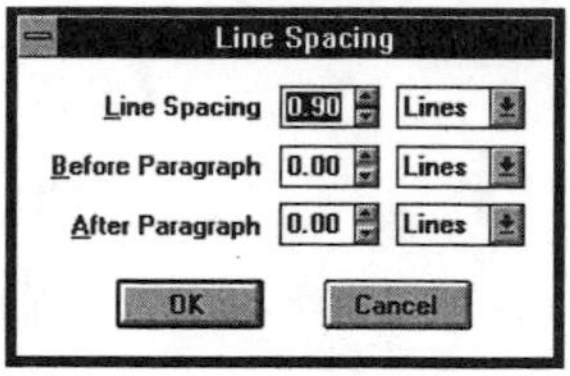

Figure 6.5   The Line Spacing dialog box.

In this lesson, you learned how to add labels and basic text objects to a slide, as well as how to change the text alignment and line spacing. In the next lesson, you will learn how to use tabs and indents to create columns and lists.

Creating Columns and Lists

In this lesson, you will learn how to use tabs to create columns of text and indents to create bulleted lists, numbered lists, and other types of lists.

Using Tabs to Create Columns

A presentation often uses tabbed columns to display information. For example, you may use tabs to create a three-column list like the one shown in Figure 7.1.

In addition to hardware products, we carry a varied line of software:		
Business	**Home**	**Education**
WordPerfect	Quicken	Reader Rabbit 2
Microsoft Word	The New Print Shop	Oregon Trail
PowerPoint	Microsoft Works	BodyWorks
Excel	TurboTax	Where in the World is Carmen Sandiego?

Figure 7.1 You can use tabs to create a multi-column list.

To set the tabs for such a list, perform the following steps:

1. Select the text object for which you want to set the tabs.

2. Click inside the paragraph whose tabs you want to set, or select two or more paragraphs.

3. Open the Text menu and select Show Ruler. The ruler appears above the text box.

4. Move the mouse pointer over the icon for the type of tab you want to set:

    Aligns the left end of the line against the tab stop.

   Centers the text on the tab stop.

   Aligns the right end of the line against the tab stop.

   Aligns the tab stop on a period. This is useful for aligning a column of numbers that use decimal points.

5. Hold down the mouse button and drag the icon below the ruler to where you want to set the tab stop (see Figure 7.2).

6. Repeat steps 4 and 5 for each tab stop you want to set.

7. To change the position of an existing tab stop setting, drag it on the ruler to the desired position. To delete an existing tab stop setting, drag it off the ruler.

8. Open the Text menu and select Hide Ruler.

Turning the Ruler On and Off   To turn the ruler on or off quickly, press Ctrl+R.

Drag a tab marker. ─────────

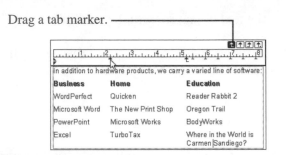

Figure 7.2 The ruler lets you enter and change tab stop settings.

Using Indents to Create Lists

Indents allow you to indent one or more lines of a paragraph from the left margin. You have already seen indents used in the Master Body to create a bulleted list. You can use indents in any text object to create a similar list, or your own custom list.

To indent existing text, perform the following steps:

1. Select the text object that contains the text you want to indent.

2. Click inside the paragraph whose indents you want to set, or select two or more paragraphs.

3. Open the Text menu and select Show **R**uler. The ruler appears above the text box.

4. Drag one of the indent markers (as shown in Figure 7.3) to set the indents for the paragraph:

   Drag the top marker to indent the first line.

Drag the bottom marker to indent all subsequent lines.

Drag the line between the top and bottom markers to indent all the text.

5. Open the Text menu and select Hide Ruler.

Top marker controls first line.   Drag the midline marker
                                          to move both indents.

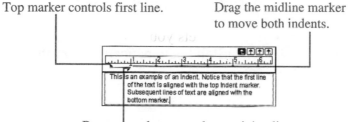

Bottom marker controls remaining lines.

Figure 7.3   Drag the indent markers to indent your text.

You can create up to five levels of indents within a single text box. To add an indent level, click on the Demote button in the Toolbox or press Alt+Shift+→. A new set of indent markers appears, showing the next level of indents. You can change these new indent settings as explained above.

Once you have set your indents, you can create a numbered or bulleted list by performing the following steps:

1. Type a number and a period, or type the character you want to use for the bullet.

2. Press the Tab key to move to the second indent mark.

3. Type the text you want to use for this item. As you type, the text is wrapped to the second indent mark, as shown in Figure 7.4.

Quick Bullets To enter a bullet quickly, click on the Bullet button in the Toolbox. This inserts a dot and a tab, so all you have to do is type the text.

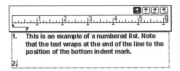

1. This is an example of a numbered list. Note that the text wraps at the end of the line to the position of the bottom indent mark.

2.

Figure 7.4 PowerPoint automatically wraps the text for you.

Changing the Bullet Character

By default, whenever you click on the Bullet button in the Toolbox to insert a bullet, PowerPoint inserts a large dot for the bullet. However, you can change the appearance of the bullet at any time by performing the following steps:

1. Select the paragraph(s) in which you want to change the bullet character.

2. Open the Text menu and select Bullet. The Bullet dialog box appears, as shown in Figure 7.5.

3. Pull down the Bullets From list, and select the character set from which you want to choose a bullet. The dialog box displays the characters in the selected set.

4. Click on the character you want to use for the bullet.

5. To set the size of the bullet, use the up and down arrows to the right of the Size text box.

6. To select a color for the bullet, pull down the Special Color drop-down list and select the desired color.

7. Select the OK button. The bullet character is changed for all selected paragraphs.

Select this box to turn bullets on or off.

Select the bullet set you want to choose from.

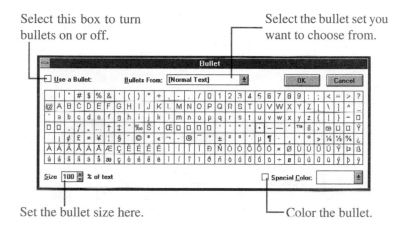

Set the bullet size here.

Color the bullet.

Figure 7.5   Use the Bullet dialog box to select a bullet character.

Changing the Indents and Bullets on the Slide Master

The Master Body on the Slide Master contains a template for creating a bulleted list on each slide. You can change the indents and bullet characters used in this template to change them for all subsequent slides. To do this, perform the following steps:

1. Open the View menu and select Slide Master. The Slide Master appears.

2. Click on the Master Body object to select it, and then press F2 to select all the paragraphs.

3. Open the Text menu and select Show Ruler. The ruler appears at the top of the Master Body object, as shown in Figure 7.6.

45

4. Change any of the indents as described earlier in this lesson.

5. Click inside the paragraph whose bullet character you want to change, and then change the character as explained earlier in this lesson.

6. Click on the Slide view button to return to Slide view.

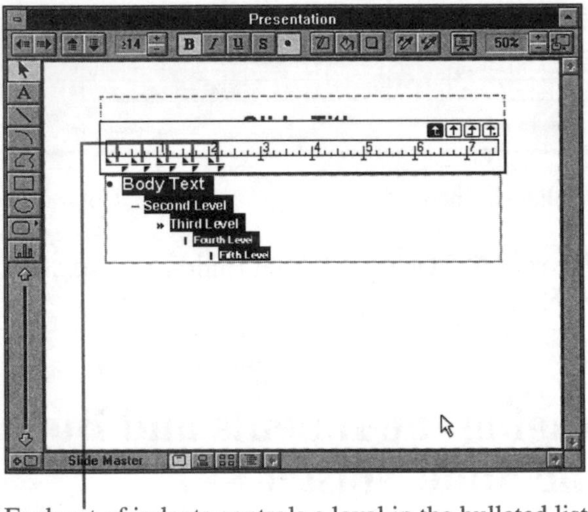

Each set of indents controls a level in the bulleted list.

Figure 7.6   Change the indents in the Master Body to change the indents for the Body text in all slides.

The changes you made to the Master Body will now affect the bulleted lists you create in the Body text object on every slide.

In this lesson, you learned how to create columns with tabs, create lists with indents, and change the bullet character for bulleted lists. In the next lesson, you will learn how to change the style, size, and color of text.

Lesson 8
Changing the
Look of the Text

In this lesson, you will learn how to change the appearance of text by changing its font, style, size, and color.

Changing Fonts

In PowerPoint, a *font* is a family of text that has the same design or *typeface* (for example, Arial or Courier). You can change the font of existing text by performing the following steps:

1. To change the font for existing text, select the text. (If you change fonts without selecting text, the selected font becomes the default font for any text you type in the presentation.)

2. Open the Text menu and select Font. The Font submenu appears, as shown in Figure 8.1.

3. Select the font you want to use. If you selected text, the selected text appears in the new font. If you did not select text, when you type the text it will appear in the selected font.

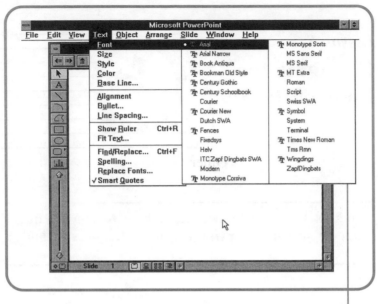

Font submenu

Figure 8.1   The Font submenu displays the fonts you can use.

Title and Body Text   Do not change fonts for Title or Body text on individual slides. If you do this, you override the font selections in the Slide Master, and risk making the slides in your presentation inconsistent. Later in this lesson, you will learn how to change the appearance of text on the Slide Master.

Changing the Size of Text

PowerPoint allows you to keep the design of the text the same while changing its size. Text size is measured in points; there are approximately 72 points in an inch.

To change the size of text, perform the following steps:

1. To change the size of existing text, select the text.

2. Open the Text menu and select Size. The Size submenu appears.

3. Select the size you want to use. To specify a size not on the submenu, select Other, type the size you want to use, and press Enter. The selected text appears in the specified size.

Use the Text Size Buttons. A quick way to change the size of text is to select the text and use the text size buttons in the Toolbox:

Click on the + button to increase the text size or click on the - button to decrease it.

Styling Your Text

In addition to fonts and sizes, you can add *styles* (including bold and italics) to your text in order to emphasize it. When you add a style to the text, its font and size remain the same, but the appearance of the text is changed. To add a style, perform the following steps:

1. To change the style of existing text, select the text.

2. Open the Text menu and select Style. The Style submenu appears, as shown in Figure 8.2.

3. Select the style you want to use. If you selected text, the selected text appears in the new style. If you did not select text, when you type the text it will appear in the selected style.

√Plain	Ctrl+T
Bold	Ctrl+B
Italic	Ctrl+I
Underline	Ctrl+U
Shadow	
Emboss	
Supe**r**script	
Sub**s**cript	

Figure 8.2 The Style submenu displays the available styles.

Use the Text Style Buttons. A quick way to change the style of text is to select the text and use one of the style buttons in the Toolbox:

Click on a button to turn the style on or off.

Changing the Text Color

The procedure for changing text color is very similar to the procedure for selecting a font, size, or style. Perform the following steps:

1. To change the color of existing text, select the text.

2. Open the Text menu and select Color. The Color submenu appears.

3. Select a color from the submenu or select Other Color. If you selected a color from the list, the text appears in

the specified color. If you selected Other Color, the Other Color dialog box appears, as shown in Figure 8.3.

4. If you chose Other Color, select a color from the dialog box, and then click on the OK button.

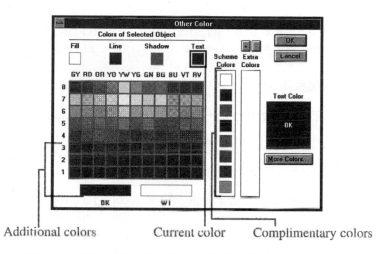

Additional colors   Current color   Complimentary colors

Figure 8.3   Use the Other Color dialog box to select a color that is not in the current color scheme.

Watch Those Color Schemes   The colors listed on the Color submenu complement the background colors in the template. If you choose an "other" color, you risk using one that will clash with the background colors and make your slides look inconsistent.

Formatting Text on the Slide Master

The Master Title and Master Body on the Slide Master contain the font, size, style, and color settings for the title and body text on each slide. You can change the settings on the Slide Master to change them for all subsequent slides. To do this, perform the following steps:

1. Open the View menu and select Slide Master. The Slide Master appears.

2. Select the text in the Master Title or Master Body object whose font, size, style, or color you want to change.

3. Change any of the text attributes as desired.

4. Click on the Slide view button to return to Slide view.

The changes you made to the Master Body will now affect the Title text and Body text on each slide you create.

In this lesson, you learned how to change the appearance of text by changing its font, size, style, and color. In the next lesson, you will learn how to draw objects on a slide.

Lesson 9

Drawing Objects on a Slide

In this lesson, you will learn how to use PowerPoint's drawing tools to draw graphic objects on a slide.

PowerPoint's Drawing Tools

PowerPoint's drawing tools are displayed along the left side of the Presentation window. The general procedure for drawing an object is to click on a tool, and then use the mouse to drag the shape to the desired size and dimensions. The following sections provide instructions for using each tool.

Drawing a Line

The *Line tool* lets you draw a straight line. To draw a line, perform the following steps:

1. Click on the Line tool.

2. Move the mouse pointer to where you want the end or center of the line to start.

3. (Optional) While drawing the line, hold down one or both of the following keys:

   Ctrl to draw the line out from a center point.

   Shift to make sure the line is horizontal, vertical, or at a 90-degree angle.

4. Hold down the mouse button and drag the mouse to draw your line.

5. Release the mouse button.

6. To add an arrow tip to the line, open the Object menu, select Arrowheads, and select the desired arrow tip.

 **Changing the Line Thickness**   To change the thickness of a line, select the line, open the Object menu, select Line Style, and select the desired line thickness.

Drawing an Arc

The *Arc tool* lets you draw a curved line. To draw an arc, perform the following steps:

1. Click on the Arc tool.

2. Move the mouse pointer where you want the end or center of the arc to start.

3. (Optional) While drawing the arc, hold down one or both of the following keys:

Ctrl to draw the arc out from a center point.

Shift to make sure the arc is circular rather than oval.

4. Hold down the mouse button and drag the mouse to draw the arc.

5. Release the mouse button.

To change the angle of the arc, double-click on the arc, or select it and choose Edit Arc from the Edit menu. A handle appears at each end of the arc, as shown in Figure 9.1. Drag a handle to change the arc's angle.

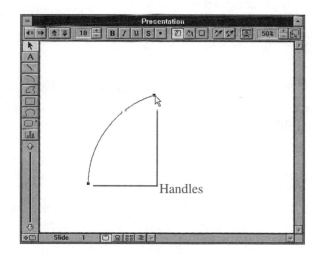

Figure 9.1   Drag a handle to change the arc's angle.

Drawing a Freeform Object

The *Freeform tool* lets you draw just as if you were using an on-screen pencil. You can draw an object made up of several straight lines (a polygon) or a freehand object.

To draw a polygon, perform the following steps:

1. Click on the Freeform tool.

2. Move the mouse pointer to where you want the object to start, and click the mouse button. This anchors the first line.

3. Move the mouse pointer (do not drag) to the place where you want the first line segment to end, and click the mouse button.

4. Continue moving the mouse pointer and clicking to add line segments to the figure.

5. To complete the polygon, perform one of the following steps:

   To create a closed shape: Click near the beginning of the first line. The end of the last line is connected to the beginning of the first line.

   To create an open shape: Press the Esc key or click outside the drawing area.

   To draw a freehand object, select the Freeform tool and then drag the mouse around on-screen to draw your lines. You can draw straight lines by releasing the mouse button and then clicking where you want the line to end, just as you did to draw a polygon. You can then return to freehand drawing by holding down the mouse button. To end the shape, press Esc or click near the beginning of the drawing.

Drawing a Rectangle or Oval

The *Rectangle* and *Oval tools* work in much the same way. To use one of these tools, perform the following steps:

1. Click on the Rectangle or Oval tool.

2. Move the mouse pointer to where you want an end (or the center) of the object to be.

3. (Optional) While drawing the object, hold down one or both of the following keys:

   Ctrl to draw the rectangle or oval out from a center point.

   Shift to draw a square or a circle.

4. Hold down the mouse button and drag the mouse to draw the object.

5. Release the mouse button.

Drawing a PowerPoint Shape

PowerPoint comes with several predrawn objects that you can add to your slides. To add one of these objects, perform the following steps:

1. Move the mouse pointer to the Shape tool and hold down the mouse button. The Shape menu appears, as shown in Figure 9.2.

2. Click on the shape you want to draw.

3. Move the mouse pointer where you want an end or the center of the shape to be.

4. (Optional) While drawing the object, hold down one or both of the following keys:

   Ctrl to draw the shape out from a center point.

   Shift to draw a shape that retains the dimensions shown on the Shape menu.

5. Hold down the mouse button and drag the mouse to draw the object.

6. Release the mouse button.

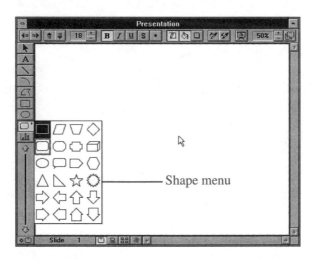

Figure 9.2   Select the desired shape from the Shape menu.

Changing an Existing Shape   You can change an existing shape into a different shape. Select the shape you want to change, open the Object menu, select Change Shape, and select the shape you want to use.

Adding Text to an Object

You can add text to a rectangle, oval, or shape, by performing the following steps:

1. Click on the object in which you want the text to appear.

2. Type the text. As you type, the text appears in a single line across the object.

3. Open the Text menu and select Fit Text. The Fit Text dialog box appears, as shown in Figure 9.3.

4. Select one of the following options to have the text included in the object:

   Adjust Object Size to Fit Text changes the size of the object to fit around the existing text.

   Word-wrap Text in Object wraps the text so it fits inside the object.

Viewing the Effects of Your Changes You can drag the title bar of the dialog box to move the dialog box away from the object. That way, you will be able to view the effects of your changes as you work.

5. Pull down the Anchor Point drop-down list and select an anchor point for the text. For example, if you select Bottom, text will sit on the bottom of the object.

6. If desired, use the Box Margins boxes to set the left, right, top, and bottom margins for your text. By increasing the margins, you force the text in toward the center of the object. By decreasing the margins, you allow the text to reach out toward the edges.

7. Click on the OK button to save your changes.

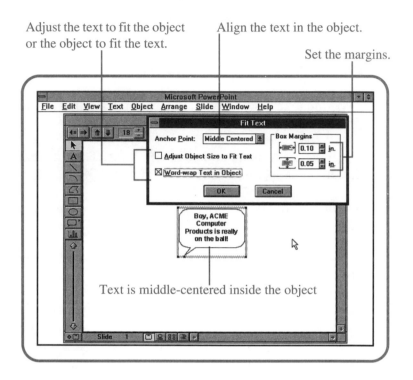

Figure 9.3 Use the Fit Text dialog box to position your text inside the object.

You can change the style and alignment of the text in an object in the same way you can change style and alignment in any text box. Refer to Lessons 6, 7, and 8 for details.

In this lesson, you learned how to use PowerPoint's drawing tools to add basic shapes and line drawings to your slides. In the next lesson, you will learn how to add PowerPoint clip art objects and other predrawn graphics to your slides.

Lesson 10
Adding Clip Art to a Slide

In this lesson, you will learn how to add PowerPoint clip art images and other pictures to a slide, and how to recolor and crop pictures.

Opening a Clip Art Library

Clip Art Clip art is a collection of previously created images or pictures that can be incorporated into a slide presentation.

PowerPoint contains several Clip Art libraries that are stored on disk as presentation files. To use a piece of clip art from one of these libraries, you must first open the desired Clip Art library by performing the following steps:

1. Open the File menu and select Open Clip Art. The Open Clip Art dialog box appears.

2. In the Directories list, make sure the C:\POWERPNT \CLIPART directory is selected. A list of clip art libraries appears in the File Name list.

3. Click on a file name in the list, or tab to the list and use the ↓ key to highlight a name. When you highlight the name of a Clip Art library, a slide appears in the preview area, showing a sample piece of clip art.

4. Press Enter or double-click on the name of the Clip Art library you want to use. PowerPoint opens a presentation window for the selected Clip Art library, and displays a list of slides in Outline view. (See Figure 10.1.)

5. Display the slide you want to use by performing either of the following steps:

   Double-click on the number to the left of the desired slide.

   Click on the Slide view button, and use the Slide Changer to display the slide.

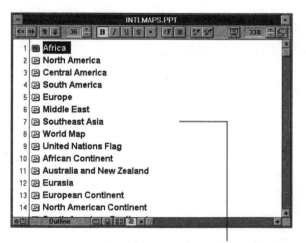

Each piece of clip art is on a separate slide.

Figure 10.1 The Clip Art library is opened as a presentation in Outline view.

Copying and Pasting a Clip Art Object

Once you have displayed the slide that contains the clip art object you want to use, you can copy the object from its slide and paste it into your slide. Perform the following steps:

1. Click on the object you want to copy. A selection box appears around the object. (See Figure 10.2.)

2. Open the Edit menu and select Copy, or press Ctrl+C. The selected object is copied to the Windows Clipboard.

3. Change to the Presentation window that contains the slide on which you want to paste the object.

4. Open the Edit menu and select Paste, or press Ctrl+V. The object is pasted from the Clipboard onto the slide.

5. Move the mouse pointer over the clip art object, hold down the mouse button, and drag the object to the desired position.

Picture Too Big?   If the picture is too big or too small, drag a corner of the picture to resize it. To retain the proportions of the picture as you resize it, hold down the Shift key while dragging.

Selection box

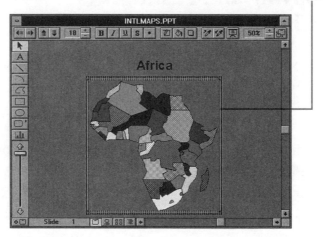

Figure 10.2 When you select the clip art object, a selection box appears around it.

Inserting Pictures Created in Other Programs

In addition to inserting clip art objects, PowerPoint allows you to insert pictures created in other graphics programs. To insert a picture, perform the following steps:

1. Open the Edit menu and select Insert. The Insert submenu appears.

2. Select Picture. The Insert Picture dialog box appears, as shown in Figure 10.3.

3. Use the Drives drop-down list to select the drive that contains the picture file.

4. Use the Directories list to change to the directory that contains the file. A list of graphics files appears in the File Name list.

5. Click on a file name in the list, or tab to the list and use the ↓ key to highlight a name.

6. To link the graphics file to this slide, select Link to File. If you make this selection, then whenever you change the file using the program you used to create it, the same changes will appear on your PowerPoint slide.

7. Click on the OK button. The picture is inserted on the slide.

8. Move the mouse pointer over the clip art object, hold down the mouse button, and drag the object to the desired position.

A list of picture files

Select the type of file, if desired.

Current directory

Figure 10.3 Use the Insert Picture dialog box to insert a picture created in another program.

Changing the Colors of a Picture

When you paste a clip art image or insert a picture on a slide, the picture appears in its original colors. These colors may clash with the colors in your presentation. To change the colors in a picture, perform the following steps:

1. Click on the picture whose colors you want to change. A selection box appears around the picture.

2. Open the Object menu and select Recolor Picture. The Recolor Picture dialog box appears, as shown in Figure 10.4.

3. Select a color you want to change in the Change From list. An x appears in the check box next to the color.

4. Use the drop-down menu to the right of the selected color to choose the color you want to change to.

 **Using the Other Option**   At the bottom of each color's drop-down menu is the Other option. Select this option if you want to use a color that is not listed on the menu.

5. Click on the Preview button to view the effects of your change.

6. Repeat steps 3 through 5 for each color you want to change.

7. Click on the OK button to put your changes into effect.

Select an existing color.⎯⎤ Select a color to change to.

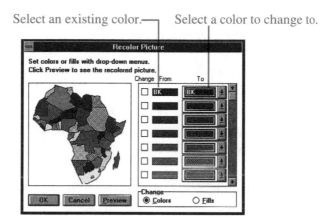

Figure 10.4 Use the Recolor Picture dialog box to change the colors in a picture.

Cropping a Picture

If you do not want to use an entire picture on your slide, you can crop the picture to use only a portion of it. To crop a picture, perform the following steps:

1. Click on the picture you want to crop. A selection box appears around the picture.

2. Open the Object menu and select Crop Picture. The mouse pointer changes into a cropping tool, as shown here:

3. Move the cropping tool over one of the picture's handles (the corner of the picture), hold down the mouse button, and drag the mouse to cut off the desired portion of the picture.

4. You can crop from other corners until only the desired portion of the picture is shown.

5. When you are done, click anywhere outside the object.

Uncropping Saves the Day   If you cut off part of a picture by mistake, you can uncrop it to reveal the part you cut off.

In this lesson, you learned how to add clip art objects and other pictures to your slides. In the next lesson, you will learn how to add a graph to a slide.

Lesson 11

Adding a
Graph to
a Slide

In this lesson you will learn how to create a graph, enter and edit data, and add it to your slide presentation.

Starting the Graph Program

PowerPoint provides an embedded graphics program called Microsoft Graph. Using Microsoft Graph, you can create a variety of graphs without ever leaving PowerPoint.

What's an Embedded Program? Embedded programs are those you can run without having to leave PowerPoint. You can create and edit objects in an embedded program like Graph, and then put those objects in PowerPoint; the objects become embedded in your presentation.

To create a graph on a slide for your presentation, perform the following steps:

1. Go to the slide to which you would like to add the graph.

2. Click on the Graphing tool.

3. Drag a box onto the slide that is the approximate size of the graph you want to create.

4. When you release the mouse button, the Microsoft Graph window will appear (as shown in Figure 11.1).

Click here to select all cells.   Legend

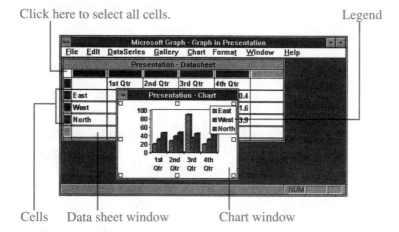

Cells   Data sheet window   Chart window

Figure 11.1   The Microsoft Graph Window.

Adding Data to the Datasheet

The *Datasheet* is set up very much like a spreadsheet with rows, columns, and cells. Each rectangle in the Datasheet is a cell which can hold text or numbers. When you enter data into the Datasheet, Graph will convert the data into a graph which is displayed in the Chart window. To enter data into the Datasheet, follow these steps:

1. Make the Datasheet window active by clicking anywhere on the window.

2. Click on the cell you want to change (or to which you want to add data), and enter the new cell information.

3. Click on the next cell to change, or use your arrow keys to move from one cell to another.

4. Repeat steps 2 and 3 until all your data is entered.

5. Activate the Chart window by clicking anywhere on the window to display the effects your data has created on the chart.

Editing the Data in the Datasheet

You may need to edit and move the data around in the Datasheet to meet your graphing needs.

Cut, Copy, Paste, and Clear Cells

You can cut, copy, paste, and clear cells in the Datasheet— one cell at a time, or as a selected group of cells. To select cells to edit, perform the following steps:

1. Place the pointer in the first cell of the group to select.

2. Click and hold the mouse button.

3. Drag the pointer over the remainder of cells to be selected, and release the button.

Quick Select   Select an entire row or column by clicking on the black rectangle above the column (or to the left of the row).

4. Open the Edit menu and select either Cut, Copy, Paste, or Clear.

Select All   To select every cell in the Datasheet, open the Edit menu and select Select All or click on the upper-leftmost square in the Datasheet (see Figure 11.1).

Deleting Rows and Columns

You can delete any unwanted rows and columns in the Datasheet. To delete, perform the following steps:

1. Click on any cell in the row or column you want to delete.

2. Open the Edit menu and select Delete Row/Col.

3. In the Delete Row/Col dialog box, select Delete Rows or Delete Columns.

4. Click on OK to delete the row or column.

Inserting Rows and Columns

You can insert a blank row or column into the Datasheet pushing aside the rows and columns. To insert, perform the following steps:

1. Click on the row or column you want to push over one column or down one row.

2. Open the Edit menu and select Insert Row/Col.

3. In the Insert Row/Col dialog box, select Insert Rows or Insert Columns.

4. Click on OK to insert the row or column.

Changing Column Width

There may be times when the data entry you make in a Datasheet cell is too long and you will need to adjust the width of the column. To change the column width, perform the following steps:

1. Select the columns or cells you want to adjust.

2. Open the Format menu and select Column Width.

3. In the Column Width dialog box, type a number from 1 to 255 (as shown in Figure 11.2).

Standard Width The standard width is 9. Click on the Standard Width box to revert to the standard column width.

4. Click on OK to save your changes.

Quick Width Adjustment Place the pointer between the black rectangles above the columns. Hold down the mouse button and drag the line to adjust the column width.

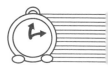

Click here to adjust column width.

Microsoft Graph - Graph in Presentation						
File Edit DataSeries Gallery Chart Format Window Help						

Presentation - Datasheet

	1st Qtr	2nd Qtr	3rd Qtr	4th Qtr	
East	20.4	27.4	90	20.4	
West	30.6	38.6	34.6	31.6	
North	45.9		**Column Width**		

Column Width: 9   OK
☐ Standard Width   Cancel

NUM

Figure 11.2   The Column Width dialog box.

Adding the Graph to the Slide

To add the graph to the slide, perform the following steps:

1. Open the File menu and select Exit and Return to Presentation (see Figure 11.3).

2. Click on the OK button. The graph is added to the slide.

Return to Graph   To edit a graph once it has been added to a slide, double-click on the graph to return to Microsoft Graph window.

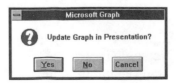

Microsoft Graph

❓ Update Graph in Presentation?

Yes   No   Cancel

Figure 11.3   Click on OK to add the graph to the slide.

74

In this lesson, you learned how to create a graph, enter and edit data, and add the graph to a slide. In the next lesson, you will learn how to modify and edit the graph.

Editing Your Graph

In this lesson, you will learn how to edit and enhance your graphs for the slide presentation.

Editing a Graph from PowerPoint

After you have added a graph to your PowerPoint slide presentation, you can edit that graph as many times as you like. You can move, copy and paste, and display your Datasheet data in many different types of graphs, and colors.

Moving the Graph on the Slide

You can move the position of the graph on the slide by performing the following steps:

1. Click anywhere on the graph.

2. Drag the graph to a different position on the slide.

Copy and Paste a Graph

You can copy a graph from one slide to another in the same presentation, or to another presentation.

1. Click anywhere on the graph.

2. Open the Edit menu and select Copy.

3. Click on the Slide Changer to select the slide to copy the graph to.

4. Open the Edit menu and select Paste. A duplicate graph is pasted into the slide.

Changing Graph Types

You can change the way your Datasheet data is displayed by changing the graph type. To select a different graph type, perform the following steps:

1. Double-click on the graph in the slide.

2. Open the Gallery menu and select one of the twelve graph types of your choice. For example, click on 3-D Pie and the dialog box shown in Figure 12.1 appears.

3. Click on one of the graph types.

4. Click on OK to apply the graph types to your data.

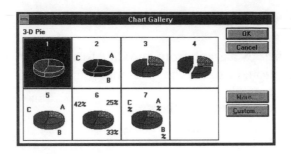

Figure 12.1   The 3-D Pie Chart Gallery dialog box.

Changing Graph Colors

You can apply different colors and patterns to the elements of a graph by performing the following steps:

1. Double-click on the graph in the slide.

2. Open the Format menu and select Color Palette.

3. The Color Palette dialog box appears, as shown in Figure 12.2.

4. The current default colors are listed. To alter any of these colors, click on the color you want to change.

5. Click on the Edit button.

6. To adjust the amount of color, hue, saturation, and luminosity, click on the up or down arrows in the color control boxes. (These are labeled Color/Solid, Hue, Sat, Lum; see the right half of Figure 12.2.)

7. When you have the color you want, click on the OK button.

8. Repeat steps 5 through 7 to change any other colors in the palette.

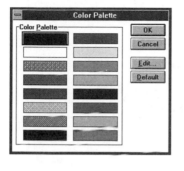
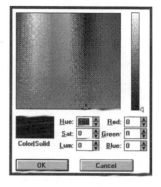

Figure 12.2 Changing the colors of the graph.

Editing Legends

The *legend* provides a guide to each color, pattern, or symbol represented on the graph. You can add, delete, or move the legend, and format its font, color, style and borders.

Adding a Legend

You can add a legend to the graph by performing the following steps:

1. Double-click on the graph in the slide.

2. Open the Chart menu and select Add Legend.

There is no Add Legend If you already have a legend on the graph, the Chart menu will not have the Add Legend menu option available.

Deleting a Legend

To delete a legend, perform the following steps:

1. Double-click on the graph in the slide.

2. Open the Chart menu and select Delete Legend.

Quick Delete To delete a legend quickly, select it by clicking anywhere on the legend, and pressing the Delete key.

Once you delete a legend, the Delete Legend command on the Chart menu changes to Add Legend.

Moving a Legend

If you don't like the placement of the legend on the Chart window, you can move it by performing the following steps:

1. Double-click on the graph in the slide.

2. Click on the legend in the Chart window.

3. Drag the box to the new position in the Chart Window.

Formatting a Legend

You can change the appearance of the information in the legend by performing the following steps.

1. Double-click on the graph in the slide.

2. Click on the legend in the Chart Window.

3. Open the Format menu and select Patterns. The Area Patterns dialog box will appear (as shown in Figure 12.3).

4. To adjust the border style, color, and line weight, choose an option from the drop-down lists.

5. To adjust the pattern, foreground color, and background color, choose an option from the drop-down lists.

6. To format the legend text font, click on the Font button and select an option.

7. To reposition the legend, click on the Legend button and select an option.

8. Click on OK to save changes.

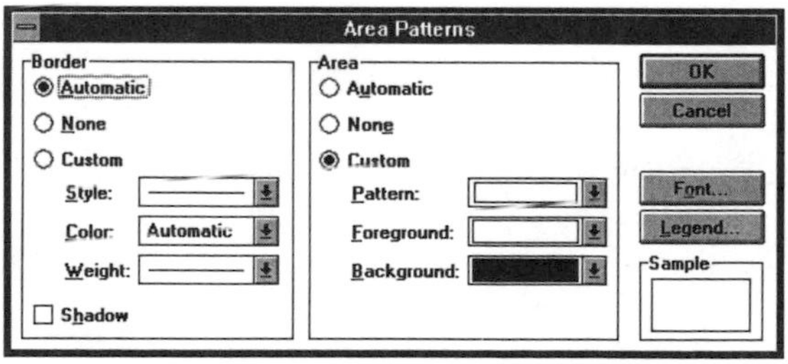

Figure 12.3   The Area Patterns dialog box.

In this lesson, you learned how to move and copy graphs, select different graph types, adjust colors, and work with legends. In the next lesson, you will learn how to position and size objects on a slide.

Lesson 13
Editing, Moving, and Sizing Objects

In this lesson, you will learn how to edit, move, and resize objects on the slide presentation.

As you may have already discovered, *objects* are the building blocks with which you create slide presentations in PowerPoint. Objects are the shapes you draw, the graphs you create, the pictures you import, and the text you type. In this and the next lesson, you will learn how to manipulate objects on your slides for impressive presentations.

Selecting Objects

You must first select an object before you can edit, copy, move, and resize an object. To select an object, perform the following steps:

1. Click on the Selection tool, as shown here:

2. Click on any part of an object. A *selection box* will surround the object selected.

 **Selecting with a Box** Another selection option is to drag a selection box around the object. This is accomplished by clicking and dragging the mouse pointer around the object to create a rectangle.

Editing Objects

There may be times when you need to edit an object. You can cut, copy, paste, and delete any object in the slide presentation.

Cutting Objects

Cutting an object from a slide deletes it and places it in the Windows Clipboard to be pasted by you elsewhere. Cut an object by performing the following steps:

1. Select an object to cut.

2. Open the Edit menu and select Cut. The object will be placed in the Clipboard.

Copying Objects

Copying an object on a slide makes a copy and places it in the Windows Clipboard; then you can paste it elsewhere. Figure 13.1 shows an object copied using the Copy and Paste commands (described in the next section). To copy an object, perform the following steps:

1. Select an object to copy.

2. Open the Edit menu and select Cut (or press Ctrl+C). The object will be placed in the Clipboard.

This object was copied...   ...then pasted here.

Figure 13.1   A copied object.

Pasting Objects

Once you have placed an object in the Windows Clipboard by cutting or copying, *pasting* will put that object back into the slide. To paste an object, follow these steps:

1. Position the pointer on your slide at the place where you want the object to appear.

2. Open the Edit menu and select Paste (or press Ctrl+V). The object will be copied from the Clipboard.

Deleting Objects

Deleting an object will remove it from the slide without placing it in the Windows Clipboard. To delete an object, perform these steps:

1. Select the object to delete.

2. Open the Edit menu and select Clear. The object will be deleted.

Quick Delete You can also delete an object from a slide by selecting it, and then pressing the Delete key.

Moving Objects

If an object is not in the correct position on a slide, you can move it to a new location by following these steps:

1. Place the pointer over the object to move.

2. Click and drag the object to a new location.

Resizing Objects

There may be times when an object you have created or imported is not the right size for your slide presentation. Resize the object by performing these steps:

1. Select the object to resize.

2. Drag one of the *resize handles* (see Figure 13.2) until the object is the desired size.

3. Release the mouse button and the object will be resized (see Figure 13.2).

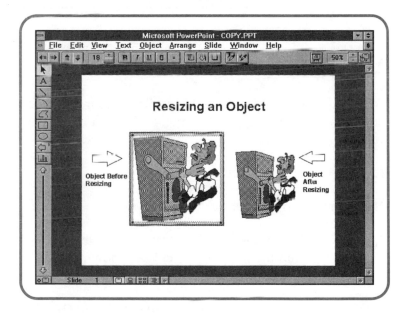

Figure 13.2 Before and after resizing an object.

In this lesson, you learned how to select, edit, move, and resize an object in a slide. In the next lesson, you will learn how to change the look of an object.

87

Changing the Look of Objects

In this lesson, you will learn how to edit the look of an object on a slide by adding borders, colors, patterns, and shadows and how to group and ungroup objects.

Adding a Frame

You can frame an object by adding a line which surrounds the shape of the object. To add a line, perform the following steps:

1. Select the object to be framed.

2. Open the Object menu and select Line.

3. Click on a line color, and a frame with the selected color will surround the selected object (as shown in Figure 14.1).

You can also click on the Line tool (see Figure 14.1) to turn a frame on or off quickly after selecting the object.

Thicken It Up You can change the thickness of the line that frames an object by selecting Line Style from the Objects menu.

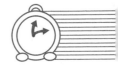

Line tool

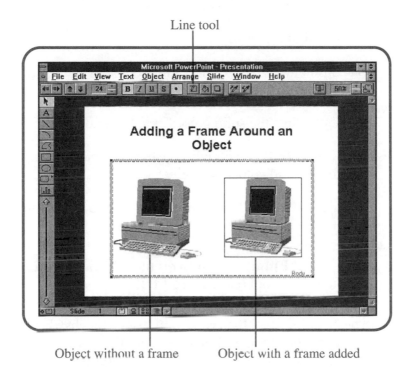

Object without a frame   Object with a frame added

Figure 14.1 A frame around an object.

Adding a Fill

Filling an object can add emphasis and texture, and make it stand out in a slide presentation (see Figure 14.2). An object can be filled with one or two colored patterns, shaded colors, or with one color and shading as the background. To fill an object, perform these steps:

1. Select an object to fill.

2. Open the Object menu and select Fill.

3. Select one of the following options:

   None   Removes a fill.

   Background   Fills with the same color as the background and shading.

   Shading   Sets the solid color fill to be shaded.

   Patterned   Fills objects with a pattern and background and foreground colors you select.

   Color Scheme   Fills an object with a solid color you select.

   **Make it Empty**   To turn off the fill quickly, click on the Fill tool (see Figure 14.2).

The Shading and Patterned options in the list have dialog boxes that appear after you select them. For more information on these dialog box options, refer to the sections that follow.

Fill tool

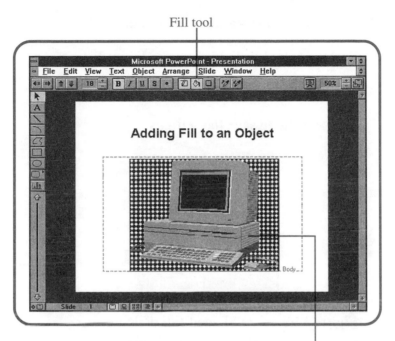

Object with colors, shading, and patterns added

Figure 14.2 An object which has been filled with colors and patterns.

Shaded Fill Dialog Box Options

After selecting Shading from the Objects Fill menu, the Shaded Fill dialog box appears (as shown in Figure 14.3). Select any of the following options:

1. Select one of the following Shade Styles: Vertical, Horizontal, Diagonal Right, Diagonal Left, From Corner, or From Center.

2. Select one of the Variants displayed.

3. Select a color by clicking on the From: list box.

4. Move the slide from Dark to Light for the color selected.

5. Click on OK to save the settings.

Figure 14.3 The Shaded Fill dialog box.

Patterned Fill Dialog Box Options

After selecting Patterned from the Objects Fill menu, the Patterned Fill dialog box appears as shown in Figure 14.4. Select any of the following options:

1. Select one of the patterns displayed in the Pattern box.

2. Select a Foreground color for the pattern from the drop-down list.

3. Select a Background color for the pattern from the drop-down list.

4. Click OK to save your settings.

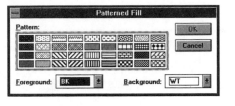

Figure 14.4   The Patterned Fill dialog box.

Adding a Shadow

Adding a shadow gives a 3-D effect to an object, as shown in Figure 14.5. To add a shadow, perform these steps:

1. Select the object to add a shadow to.

2. Open the Object menu and select Shadow.

3. Select a color for the shadow.

I Don't Want a Shadow Anymore   If an object already has a shadow, repeating these steps and selecting None will remove it.

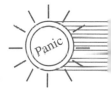

Emboss It!   To emboss an object, click on Embossed from the Objects Shadow submenu, and select a color.

After selecting the object, you can also turn a shadow on or off quickly—just click on the Shadow tool (see Figure 14.5).

93

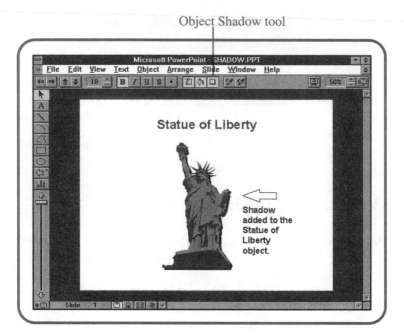

Figure 14.5 The Statue of Liberty with a shadow added.

Group and Ungroup Objects

Grouping objects combines them so you can work with them together. *Ungrouping* objects allows you to work on separate pieces of an object, to change their color, font, or size.

Grouping Objects

1. Click and drag a selection box around the objects you want to group.

2. Open the Arrange menu and select Group (or press Ctrl+G).

Ungrouping Objects

1. Select the grouped object.

2. Open the Arrange menu and select Ungroup (or press Ctrl+H).

Regrouping Objects

1. Select one of the objects that was previously grouped.

2. Open the Arrange menu and select Regroup.

In this lesson, you learned how to edit an object by adding a frame, colors, patterns, shadows, grouping, and ungrouping. In the next lesson, you will learn about adding colors to your slide presentation.

Lesson 15
Working with Colors

In this lesson, you will learn how to choose a color scheme, change and switch its colors, copy it, and apply it to other presentations.

Choosing a Color Scheme

Color schemes in PowerPoint are sets of professionally balanced colors (eight in each one), designed to be used as the primary colors in a slide presentation. Each color scheme consists of Background, Lines and Text, Shadows, Title Text, Fills, and Other Colors. Using one of these color schemes ensures that your presentation will look appealing and professional.

1. Open the Slide menu and select Color Scheme. The Color Scheme dialog box appears (as shown in Figure 15.1).

2. Choose the Choose a Scheme button. The Choose a Scheme dialog box appears (as shown in Figure 15.2).

3. Select a Background color.

4. Select a Text color.

5. Select the Remaining Colors.

6. Click on OK when finished selecting colors. The Color Scheme dialog box reappears. (See Figure 15.1.)

7. Choose one of the options in the Apply To box. One will apply the selected colors only to the current slide on-screen; the other applies them to all slides in the presentation.

8. Click on OK to save the color scheme.

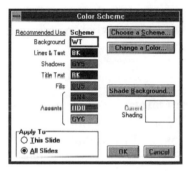

Figure 15.1 The Color Scheme dialog box.

Figure 15.2 The Choose a Scheme dialog box.

Changing a Color Scheme

You can modify any color in a color scheme to create your own custom combinations. For example, you can create your own color combinations that match your company colors or logo. To change a color scheme, perform the following steps:

1. Open the Slide menu and select Color Scheme.

2. Click on a color in the scheme to be changed.

3. Choose the Change a Color button. The Change a Color dialog box appears, as shown in Figure 15.3.

4. Select a color.

 **Custom Colors** To create a custom color, click on the More Colors button, and adjust the Hue, Saturation, and Luminance.

5. Click on OK to change the color and return to the Color Scheme dialog box.

6. Repeat steps 2 through 5 to change any other colors.

7. When finished changing colors, click on OK.

Switching Colors in the Scheme

If you don't like the location of a color in the color scheme, you can switch it with another color by performing the following steps:

1. Open the Slide menu and select Color Scheme.

2. Click and drag to switch a color in the scheme to a new location.

3. Select an option in the Apply to box.

4. Click on OK to change the switch.

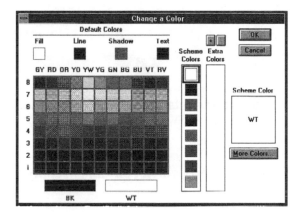

Figure 15.3 The Change a Color dialog box.

Copying and Applying a Color Scheme to Other Presentations

You can reuse a color scheme you have created in one presentation by copying it and applying it to another presentation. This is particularly useful if you have created a custom color scheme. To copy a color scheme from one presentation to another, perform these steps:

1. To open the presentation that contains the color scheme you want to copy, open the File menu and select Open.

2. Open the View menu and select Slide Sorter, or click on the Slide Sorter button as shown here:

3. Select the slide which contains the color scheme you want to copy.

4. Open the Edit menu and select Pick Up Scheme, or click on the Pick Up Scheme tool as shown here:

5. Change to the presentation to which you want to copy your chosen color scheme by opening the File menu and selecting Open.

6. Select the slide(s) to which you want to apply the color scheme.

Selecting Multiple Slides You can select more than one slide by holding down the Shift key as you select a slide.

7. Open the Edit menu and select Apply Scheme, or click on the Apply Scheme tool as shown here:

In this lesson, you learned how to choose, change, switch, and copy a color scheme to other presentations. In the next lesson, you will learn how to add final touches to the Slide Master.

Lesson 16

Adding Final Touches to the Slide Master

In this lesson, you will learn how to add background items such as art, text, date, time, and page numbers to the Slide Master.

Background Items

Background items you add to the Slide Master appear on every slide and printed page, to add consistency to your slide presentation. You can add background items such as shapes, text, date, time, page numbers, and pictures.

Adding Pictures

You can add pictures, graphics, and art to the background so it appears on each slide. For example, you can have your company logo (or graphics representing your company, department, or project) displayed on each slide. (See Figure 16.1.) To add pictures to the background of the Slide Master, follow these steps:

1. Open the View menu and select Slide Master.

2. Create (draw), paste, or insert a picture or graphics into the Slide Master.

3. Move the picture to where you want it to appear on every slide.

Adding Text

You can add text to the Slide Master that you want to appear on every slide. For example, you can add the presentation's title, the company or project name, or the author's name (see Figure 16.1). To add text to the background of the Slide Master, perform these steps:

1. Open the View menu and select Slide Master.

2. Click the Text tool as shown here:

3. Click where you want the text to appear on the slide.

4. Type the text.

5. (Optional) Change the font, size, or color of the text.

Adding Date, Time, or Page Number

PowerPoint can stamp the date, time, and page number on your slides and pages automatically, to provide a record of when you print or run a slide show. PowerPoint will substitute the date with // (slashes), the time with :: (colons), or page number with ## (pound signs).

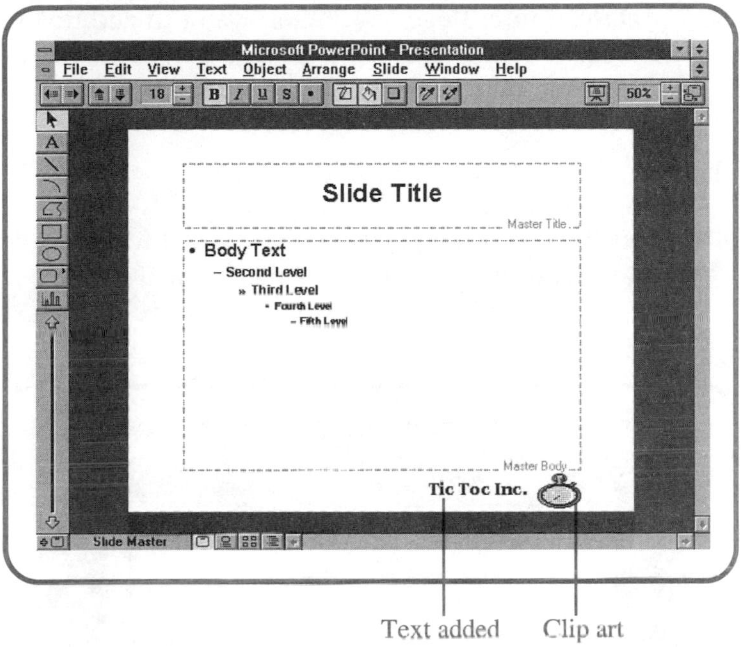

Text added   Clip art

Figure 16.1   Slide Master with clip art and text added as background items.

There are two ways to add the date, time, or page number to the Slide Master. You can use the menu or type them yourself. To add the date, time, or page number, perform the following steps:

Menu Method

1. Click on the Text tool.

2. Click where you want the information to begin on the slide.

103

 **Date, Time, Page** You may want to add text to precede the date, time, and page number symbols (for example, `Page Number` or `Date Printed`).

3. Open the Edit menu and select Insert.

4. Select the date/time/page number to add to the Slide Master. The place-holding characters will be placed where you specified, as shown in Figure 16.2.

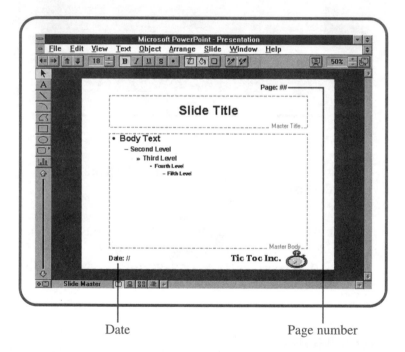

Date   Page number

Figure 16.2 The date and page number added to the Slide Master.

Input Method

1. Click on the Text tool.

2. Click where you want the information to begin on the slide.

3. Type / / for the date, : : for the time, or ## for the page number.

In this lesson, you learned how to add pictures, text, date, time, or page numbers to the Slide Master so these will appear automatically on every slide in the presentation. In the next lesson, you will learn how to rearrange slides in the presentation.

Lesson 17

Rearranging the Order of Slides

In this lesson, you will learn how to rearrange the order of your slides in the presentation.

There may be times when you will need to rearrange the sequence of slides you have created in the presentation. In PowerPoint, you are given the ability to reorder the slides in either Slide Sorter view or Outline view.

Rearranging in Slide Sorter

Slide Sorter view shows miniature versions of the slides in your presentation. This allows you to view many of your slides at one time. To rearrange the slides in Slide Sorter view, perform the following steps:

1. Click on the Slide Sorter view button, as shown here:

2. Click and drag the slide you want to move to a new location.

Get a Bigger Picture   To enlarge the slides so you can see more detail on the slide, click on the Zoom In (+) button. Note, however, that you cannot move to a slide while you are zoomed.

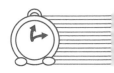

Rearranging in Outline View

The Outline view arranges your slides with title and body text displayed, allowing an overview of the slides in your presentation. To change the order of the slides in Outline view, follow these steps:

1. Click on the Outline View button, as shown here:

2. Select the slide you want to move by clicking either on the slide number or the slide icon.

One at a Time   You don't necessarily have to move an entire slide in the presentation. You can move only the slide's data—from one slide to another—by selecting only what you want to move, and dragging it to its new location.

3. Click on the Move Up or Move Down arrows, as shown here:

   or drag the slide to its new position.

   In this lesson, you learned how to rearrange the slides in a presentation, in either the Slide Sorter or Outline view. In the next lesson, you will learn how to delete, copy, and add slides to a presentation.

107

Deleting, Copying, and Adding Slides

In this lesson, you will learn how to delete, copy, or add a slide to your presentation.

Most people don't create a perfect slide presentation on the first try. PowerPoint gives you the capability of making changes—such as adding, copying, pasting, and deleting slides—after you have created the slide presentation.

Deleting Slides

To delete a slide you no longer need, you can use the Slide view, Notes view, Outline view, or Slide Sorter view. Perform the following steps, from any of these views, to delete a slide:

1. Select the slide to delete.

2. Open the Slide menu and select Delete Slide. The selected slide will be deleted.

More Than One   In the Outline and Slide Sorter views, you can select more than one slide by pressing the Shift key as you select slides.

Oops! If you delete a slide accidentally—*before you do anything else*—open the Edit menu and select Undo.

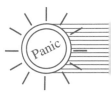

Cutting, Copying and Pasting Slides

There are times when you see changes that need to be made to better organize your slide presentation. To cut, copy, and paste a slide, perform the following steps:

1. Depending on the view you are in, select the slide you want to cut or copy.

2. Open the Edit menu and select Cut or Copy.

3. Click in front of the slide that occupies the place where you want to insert the cut or copied slide.

4. Open the Slide menu and select Paste. PowerPoint will paste the slide into its new location (see Figure 18.1).

Adding Slides

You can insert a new slide into an existing presentation. To add a new slide, perform these steps:

1. Open the Slide menu and select New Slide or click on the New Slide button.

2. A new slide will appear (see Figure 18.2).

Pasted slide   Copied slide

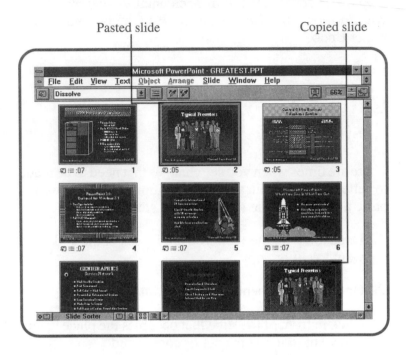

Figure 18.1 A slide copied and pasted in Slide Sorter view.

New Slide Quick The shortcut key combination for a new slide is Ctrl+N. A new slide will appear in all views. In Slide view and Slide Sorter, the new slide will become the selected slide.

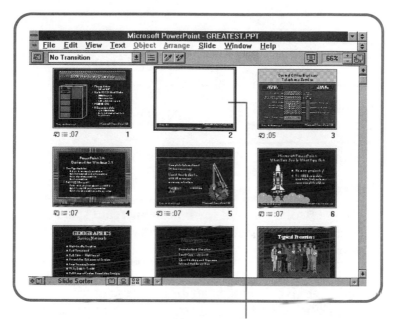

New slide added to presentation

Figure 18.2 A new slide added in Slide Sorter view.

In this lesson, you learned how to delete, copy, and add slides to a presentation. In the next lesson, you will learn how to add speaker's notes to your presentation.

Creating Speaker's Notes Pages

In this lesson, you will learn how to create speaker's notes to help you during the delivery of your presentation.

PowerPoint gives you the capability of creating *speaker's notes* to correspond to each slide in your presentation. These can be your own personal notes, and they can help in the delivery of your presentation. They can enhance the effectiveness of your slides with greater emphasis and more efficient communication.

At the top of each *notes page* is a reduced image of the slide. You can refer to it during the presentation, so it's easier to keep your place. Your personal notes appear below the image, as shown in Figure 19.1.

Creating Speaker's Notes

To create a speaker's notes, you must change to Notes view, select the Body object, and enter your notes. To create the speaker's notes, perform the following steps:

1. Click on the Slide Changer to move to the slide you want to add a note to.

2. Open the View menu and select Notes or click on the Notes View button, as shown here:

3. The Notes window will look similar to Figure 19.1. Check to make sure you have the right slide.

4. Click on the Notes Page Body object to select it.

5. Type your notes that correspond to the slide into the slide image area.

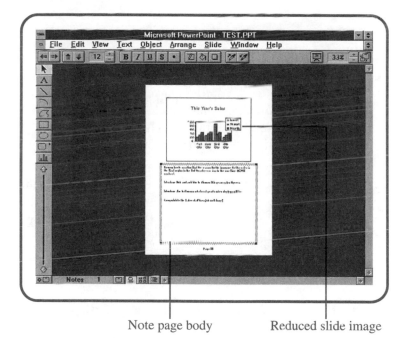

Note page body   Reduced slide image

Figure 19.1   Example of a speaker's notes page.

Printing Notes   To print out your speaker's notes, see Lesson 23 for instructions.

Changing the Size of the Slide

When you are in Notes view, the slide image at the top of the screen will appear at 33% of view. If you want to reduce or enlarge the view on the notes page, perform the following steps:

Why So Small? 33% of view means that the slide has been reduced down to 33% of its original (100%) size to fit on the notes page during a presentation.

1. In Notes view, click on the Slide Changer to move to the slide for which you want to enlarge or reduce the view.

2. Click on the View Scale + button to enlarge the size of the slide, or the − button to reduce the size, as shown here:

33%

Keep Clicking Click on the View Scale buttons as many times as needed to enlarge or reduce the size of the slide. See Figure 19.2 for a notes page which has been enlarged to 66%.

Adding Lines to the Notes Page

If you are planning to add handwritten notes later—or want to give your notes pages to your audience so they can write down ideas or further notes—you can add lines to the page (as shown in Figure 19.3). To add lines, perform these steps:

1. In Notes view, click on the Line tool.

2. Draw a line in the body.

3. Open the Edit menu and select Duplicate (or press Ctrl+D) to add more lines to the page.

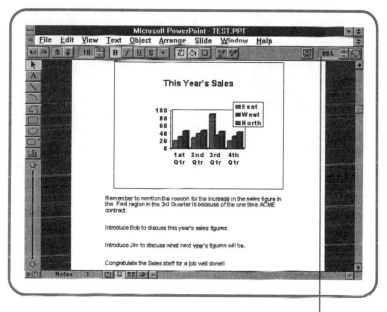

Enlarged to 66% view

Figure 19.2   A notes page enlarged to 66% view.

My Lines Don't Add Up!   When you add lines to the notes page, they are indented. To line them up any way you want, simply drag them to a new location.

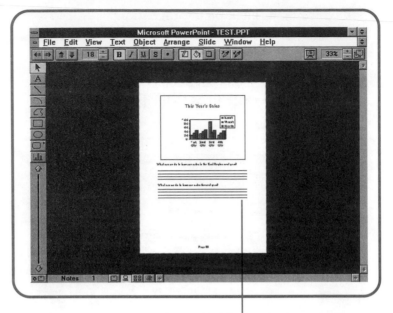

Lines added for handwritten notes

Figure 19.3   A notes page with lines added for handwritten text.

Changing the Appearance of the Notes Page

You can change the way the notes page looks by using the Notes Master. Working in the Notes Master is similar to working with the Slide Master. You can:

- Add background information (such as the date, time, or page numbers).

- Move or resize the notes page objects.

- Choose a color scheme.

- Set up the Master Body.

To change the notes page, follow these steps:

1. Open the View menu and select Notes Master, or click on the Notes View button. (This button toggles between the Notes Master and the notes page.)

2. Change any of the elements of the notes page as you would a Slide Master. See Lesson 16 for instructions.

In this lesson, you learned how to create a speaker's notes page to help in the delivery of a presentation. In the next lesson, you will learn how to create audience handouts.

Creating Audience Handouts

In this lesson, you will learn how to create audience handouts to pass out during your slide presentation.

The Handout Master

PowerPoint gives you the capability of creating handouts of the slides on your presentation. Passing these out to your audience is helpful when you have a lot of informative slides. The audience can take the slide images with them to digest in detail later.

The Handout Master has *slide image placeholders* so you can see where a slide image will be placed on a handout (see Figure 20.1). You have the choice of having two, three, or six slide images on a handout page, depending on your printer. To use the Handout Master, perform the following steps:

1. Open the View menu and select Handout Master, or click on the Slide Sorter View button (which toggles between Slide Sorter view and Handout Master) as shown here:

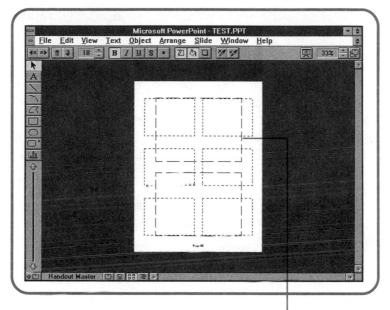

Audience Handout place holder

Figure 20.1 The Handout Master screen.

Printing Handouts To print your audience handouts, see Lesson 23 for instructions.

Changing the Appearance of Handouts

By using the Handout Master, you can change the way the audience handouts look. You can:

* Add background information (such as the date, time, or page numbers).

* Choose a color scheme.

To change the appearance of your handouts, follow these steps:

1. Open the View menu and select Handout Master, or click on the Slide Sorter button. (This button toggles between the Slide Sorter view and the Handout Master.)

2. Change any of the elements of the handout page as you would a Slide Master. (See Lesson 16 for instructions.)

In this lesson, you learned how to create audience handouts to accompany your slide presentation. In the next lesson, you will learn how to spell-check your slide presentation.

Lesson 21
Spell-Checking and Finding and Replacing Text

In this lesson, you will learn how to spell-check text in your slide presentation, and how to find and replace specific text.

Spell-checker

PowerPoint uses a built-in dictionary to spell-check your entire presentation—including all slides, outlines, note and handout pages, and all four master views. If a word is not recognized, you can add that word to a *custom dictionary*, or use a custom dictionary from other Microsoft applications. To check your spelling, perform these steps:

1. Open the Text menu and select Spelling. The Spelling dialog box appears (as shown in Figure 21.1).

2. Click on the Check Spelling button. The first misspelled word will appear, as shown in Figure 21.2.

3. Click on the Suggest button to have PowerPoint list possible correct spellings for the misspelled word.

Don't Want to Change the Spelling? If a word appears that you know is spelled correctly (like your name), and you do not want to replace it, click on the Ignore button. To add this word into your custom dictionary so PowerPoint will recognize it in the future, refer to the next section.

4. Click on the correct word in the list. Use the scroll bar to see more of the list.

5. Click the Change button to replace the misspelled word with the selected word in the slide.

Click here to start
spell-checking.

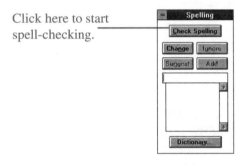

Figure 21.1 The Spelling dialog box.

Click here to
change word.

Click here for
word suggestions.

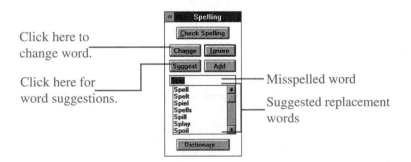

Misspelled word

Suggested replacement
words

Figure 21.2 Suggestions for a misspelled word.

Adding a Word to the Custom Dictionary

There may be times when the spell-checker does not recognize a word, and assumes it is a misspelled word. A good example of this is your name (or those of other people), company names, technical jargon, etc. To add these words to the custom dictionary, follow these steps:

1. Open the Text menu and select Spelling. The Spelling dialog box appears.

2. Click the Check Spelling button. The first misspelled word will appear.

3. When a "misspelled" word appears that you want to add to the custom dictionary, click on the Dictionary button. The Custom Dictionary dialog box will appear (as shown in Figure 21.3).

4. Click on the + button. The word will be added to the custom dictionary.

Delete from Dictionary To delete a previously added word from the custom dictionary, select the word in the list, and click on the – button.

5. Click on the Close button.

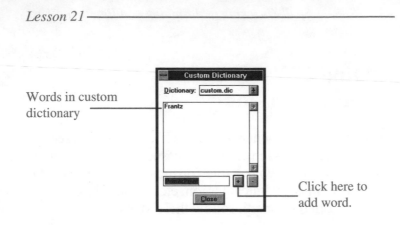

Words in custom
dictionary

Click here to
add word.

Figure 21.3   The Custom Dictionary dialog box.

Finding and Replacing Text

You can search for text and replace it in PowerPoint by
performing the following steps:

1. Open the Text menu and select Find/Replace. The
   Find/Replace text box will appear, as shown in Figure
   21.4.

2. Type the word you want to search for in the Find Text
   box.

3. (Optional) In the Replace With box, type a word to
   replace the searched word.

4. Click the Find button. PowerPoint finds the word in the
   Find Text box.

5. (Optional) Click on the Replace button.

6. Click on the Find button to find the next occurrence of
   the word.

Quick Replace To replace a word automatically and then find the next word, click on the Replace, then Find button. To replace all occurrences of the searched word automatically, and insert the replacement word without being prompted, click on the Replace All button.

Find/Replace			
Find Text: One			
Replace With: Two			
☐ Match Whole Word Only ☐ Match Case			
Find	Replace, then Find	Replace	Replace All

Figure 21.4 The Find/Replace dialog box.

In this lesson, you learned how to check your presentation for misspelled words, and how to find and replace words. In the next lesson, you will learn how to view a slide show.

Lesson 22

Viewing a Slide Show

In this lesson, you will learn how to set up and run a slide show in PowerPoint.

An electronic slide show is a lot like using a slide projector, except you can add impressive and professional visual effects (*transitions*) that move on and off the screen during the show. Slide transitions include Blinds Horizontal, Checkerboard across, Cut, and Cover Up; there are a total of 46 transitions you can choose.

Adding a Slide Transition

To apply a slide transition to a slide, perform the following steps:

1. Click on the Slide Sorter button.

2. Select the slide to which you want to add a transition effect.

3. Click on the down arrow of the Transition Effect box on the Toolbox, as shown in Figure 22.1.

More Than One To select more than one slide, hold down the Shift key while you click on slides.

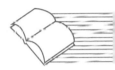

4. Click on an effect. Use the scroll bars to see more of the list.

Transition Icons PowerPoint places a *transition icon* below the lower left corner of the slide, to indicate that an effect has been applied.

Click here for rest of transitions.   Click here to run the slide show.

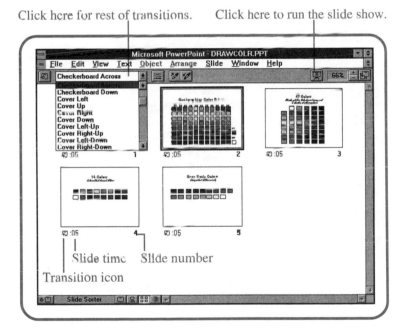

Figure 22.1 Adding transition effects to selected slides.

5. To display the slide show with the effect(s) you added, click on the Slide Show tool, as shown here:

6. Click on the mouse button or press the Spacebar to move through the slides. Press Esc to stop the slide show at any time.

Adding Timing

You can add transition effects to all the slides in your presentations, and add timing for them to move on and off the screen during the slide show. To add transitions and timing, perform the following steps:

1. Click on the Slide Sorter button.

2. Open the Edit menu and select Select All.

3. Open the Slide menu and select Transition, or click on the Transition button (on the Toolbox) as shown here:

4. The Transition dialog box appears, as shown in Figure 22.2.

5. Click the down arrow in the Effect list box.

6. Click on an effect from the list. The view box demonstrates the transition effect.

7. Click on the Slow, Medium, or Fast option button.

8. In the Advance box, click on the Only on Mouse Click option to advance a slide after you click the mouse button, or click on the Automatically After Seconds option to advance a slide after a specified amount of time.

9. If you selected **A**utomatically After Seconds, type the seconds to wait before advancing to the next slide in the presentation.

10. Click on OK.

11. To run the slide show, click on the Slide Show button.

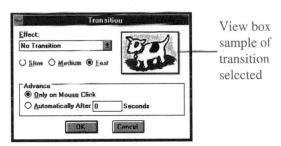

View box sample of transition selected

Figure 22.2 The Transition dialog box.

In this lesson, you learned how to create and run a slide show presentation. In the next lesson, you will learn how to print your slides, notes, and audience handouts.

Printing Slides, Outlines, Notes, and Handouts

In this lesson, you will learn how to print your slides, outlines, speaker's notes, and audience handouts.

You can use the **File Print** command to print your slides, outlines, speaker's notes, and audience handouts. The Print dialog box allows you to specify what to print, the print range, number of copies, black and white, and scale to fit paper.

Printing Slides

PowerPoint will scale your slides automatically to the printer you have selected. To print out your slides, follow these steps:

1. Open the File menu and select Print. The Print dialog box will appear, as shown in Figure 23.1.

2. Click on the Print drop-down list box.

3. Click on one of the Print Format options listed in Table 23.1.

4. Select any of the print options listed in the Print dialog box (these are listed in Table 23.2).

5. Click on OK to print.

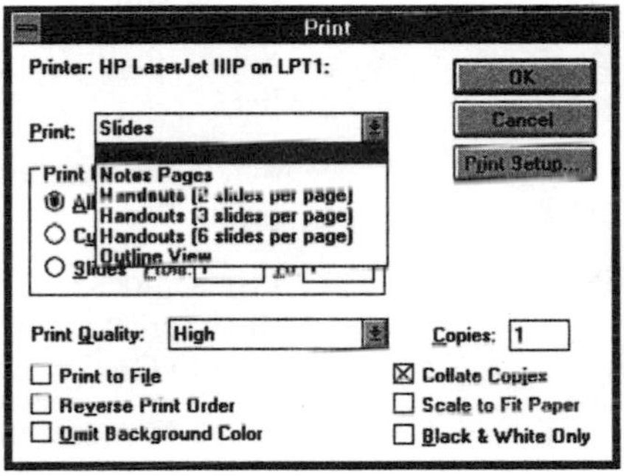

Figure 23.1 The Print dialog box.

Table 23.1 Print Format Options

Option	Description
Slides	Prints slides, one per page.
Notes Pages	Prints speaker's notes pages.
Handouts (2 slides per page)	Prints 2 slides per page.
Handouts (3 slides per page)	Prints 3 slides per page.
Handouts (6 slides per page)	Prints 6 slides per page.
Outline View	Prints outline according to view scale setting.

131

Table 23.2 Print Dialog Box Options

Option	Description
Print Range	Select a range of slides to print All, Current Slide, or Slides From: and To:
Print Quality	Select quality from drop-down list.
Copies	Select the number of copies to print.
Print to File	Prints slides to a presentation file to create 35mm slides, or to send to Genigraphics service.
Reverse Print Order	Prints from last to first page.
Omit Background Color	Prints slides, handouts, notes, and outlines without the background color.
Collate Copies	Prints multiple copies in reverse order so they are organized numerically while being printed.
Scale to Fit Paper	Scales slides automatically to fit paper size.
Black & White Only	Turns fill colors to white and text and borders to black.
Print Setup...	Click this button to select or set up a new printer.

In this lesson, you learned how to print your slides, outlines, speaker's notes, and audience handouts. Congratulations on completing the *10 Minute Guide to PowerPoint*. Have fun creating PowerPoint slide presentations.

Appendix A

Microsoft Windows Primer

Microsoft Windows is an interface program that makes your computer easier to use by enabling you to select menu items and pictures rather than type commands. Before you can take advantage of it, however, you must learn some Windows basics.

Starting Microsoft Windows

To start Windows, do the following:

1. At the DOS prompt, type win.

2. Press Enter.

The Windows title screen appears for a few moments, and then you see a screen like the one in Figure A.1.

What If It Didn't Work? You may have to change to the windows directory before starting Windows; to do so, type CD \WINDOWS and press Enter.

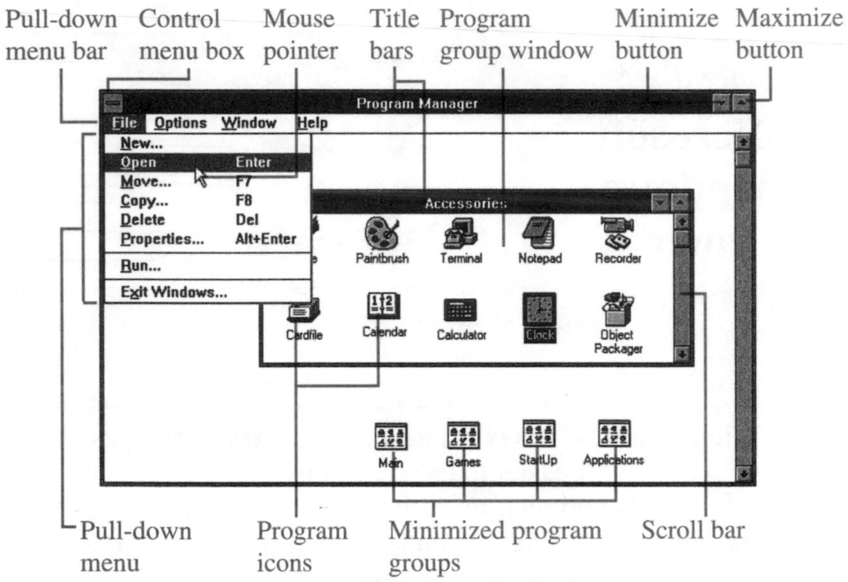

Pull-down Control   Mouse   Title Program   Minimize Maximize
menu bar   menu box pointer bars group window   button   button

Pull-down   Program   Minimized program   Scroll bar
menu   icons   groups

Figure A.1   The Windows Program Manager.

Parts of a Windows Screen

As shown in Figure A.1, the Windows screen contains
several unique elements that you won't see in DOS. Here's
a brief summary.

- *Title bar*   This shows the name of the window or
  program.

- *Program group windows*   These contain *program
  icons*, which allow you to run programs.

- *Icons*   These small pictures are graphic representa-
  tions of programs. To run a program, you select its icon.

- *Minimize and Maximize buttons* These alter a window's size. The Minimize button shrinks the window to the size of an icon. The Maximize button expands the window to fill the screen. When maximized, a window contains a double-arrow *Restore button*, which returns the window to its original size.

- *Control menu box* When selected, this pulls down a menu that offers size and location controls for the window.

- *Pull-down menu bar* This contains a list of the pull-down menus available in the program.

- *Mouse Pointer* If you are using a mouse, the mouse pointer (usually an arrow) appears on-screen. It can be controlled by moving the mouse (discussed later in this appendix).

- *Scroll bars* If a window contains more information than can be displayed in the window, a scroll bar appears. *Scroll arrows* on each end of the scroll bar allow you to scroll slowly. The *scroll box* allows you to scroll more quickly. To use either one, click on it and hold down the mouse button (see the next section for details).

Using a Mouse

To work most efficiently in Windows, you should use a mouse. You can press mouse buttons and move the mouse in various ways to change the way it acts:

Point means to move the mouse pointer onto the specified item by moving the mouse. The tip of the mouse pointer must be touching the item.

Click on an item means to move the pointer onto the specified item and press the mouse button once. Unless specified otherwise, use the left mouse button.

Double-click on an item means to move the pointer onto the specified item and press and release the mouse button twice quickly.

Drag means to move the mouse pointer onto the specified item, hold down the mouse button, and move the mouse while holding down the button.

Figure A.2 shows how to use the mouse to perform common Windows activities, such as running applications and moving and resizing windows.

Click to control window size and location.   Drag title bar to move window.   Click to minimize.   Click to maximize.

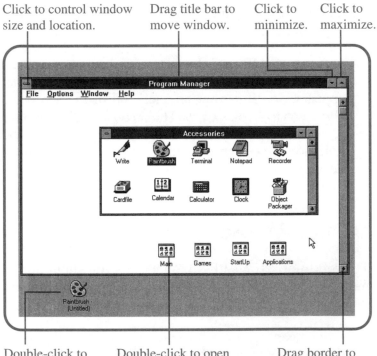

Double-click to restore application.   Double-click to open program group window.   Drag border to size window.

Figure A.2   Use your mouse to control Windows.

Starting a Program

To start a program, simply select its icon. If its icon is contained in a program group window that's not open at the moment, open the window first. Follow these steps:

1. If necessary, open the program group window that contains the program you want to run. To open a program group window, click on its icon.

2. Double-click on the icon for the program you want to run.

Using Menus

The pull-down menu bar (see Figure A.3) contains various menus from which you can select commands. Each Windows program you run has a set of pull-down menus, as does Windows itself.

To open a menu, click on its name on the menu bar. Once a menu is open, you can select a command from it by clicking on the desired command

Accelerator Keys   Notice that in Figure A.3, some commands are followed by key names such as Enter (for the **O**pen command) or F8 (for the **C**opy command). These are called *accelerator keys*. You can use these keys to perform these commands without even opening the menu.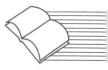

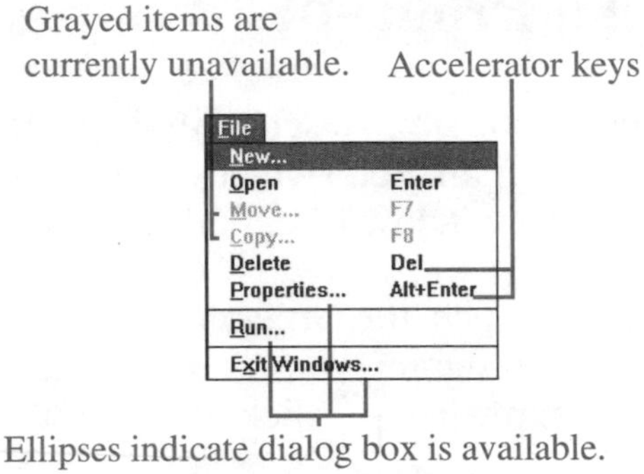

Grayed items are
currently unavailable.   Accelerator keys

Ellipses indicate dialog box is available.

Figure A.3   A menu lists various commands you
can perform.

Usually, when you select a command, it is performed
immediately. However:

- If the command name is gray (rather than black), the
  command is unavailable at the moment, and you cannot
  choose it.

- If the command name is followed by an arrow, selecting
  the command will cause another menu to appear, from
  which you select another command.

- If the command name is followed by ellipses (three
  dots), selecting it will cause a dialog box to appear.
  You'll learn about dialog boxes in the next section.

Navigating Dialog Boxes

A *dialog box* is Windows' way of requesting additional
information. For example, if you choose Properties from
the File menu, you'll see the dialog box shown in Figure
A.4.

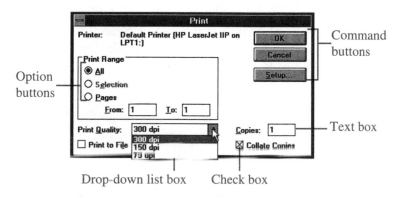

Figure A.4 A typical dialog box.

Each dialog box contains one or more of the following elements:

* *List boxes* display available choices. To activate a list, click inside the list box. If the entire list is not visible, use the scroll bar to view the items in the list. To select an item from the list, click on it.

* *Drop-down lists* are similar to list boxes, but only one item in the list is shown. To see the rest of the items, click on the down arrow to the right of the list box. To select an item from the list, click on it.

* *Text boxes* allow you to type an entry. To activate a text box, click inside it. To edit an existing entry, use the arrow keys to move the cursor, press the Del or Backspace keys to delete existing characters, and then type your correction.

* *Check boxes* allow you to select one or more items in a group of options. For example, if you are styling text, select Bold and Italic to have the text appear in both bold and italic type. Click on a check box to activate it.

139

- *Option buttons* are like check boxes, but you can select only one option button in a group. Selecting one button *deselects* any option that is already selected. Click on an option button to activate it.

- *Command buttons* execute (or cancel) the command once you have made your selections in the dialog box. To press a command button, click on it.

Switching Between Windows

Many times you will have more than one window open at once. Some open windows may be program group windows, while others may be actual programs that are running. To switch among them, you can:

- Pull down the Window menu and choose the window you want to view, or

- If a portion of the desired window is visible, click on it.

Controlling a Window

As you saw earlier in this appendix, you can minimize, maximize, and restore windows on your screen. But you can also move them and change their size.

- To move a window, drag its title bar to a different location. (Remember, "drag" means to hold down the left mouse button while you move the mouse.)

- To resize a window, position the mouse pointer on the border of the window until you see a double-headed arrow; then drag the window border to the desired size.

Copying Your Program Diskettes with File Manager

Before you install any new software, you should make a copy of the original diskettes as a safety precaution. Windows' *File Manager* makes this process easy.

First, start File Manager by double-clicking on the File Manager icon in the Main program group. Then, for each disk you need to copy, follow these steps:

1. Locate a blank disk of the same type as the original disk, and label it to match the original. Make sure the disk you select does not contain any data that you want to keep.

2. Place the original disk in your diskette drive (A or B). Remember to *write-protect* your original disks so the programs they contain will not be erased by accident.

3. Open the Disk menu and select Copy Disk. The Copy Disk dialog box appears.

4. Select the drive used in step 2 from the **S**ource In list box.

5. Select the same drive from the **D**estination In list box. (Don't worry; File Manager will tell you to switch disks at the appropriate time.)

6. Select OK. The Confirm Copy Disk dialog box appears.

7. Select Yes to continue.

8. When instructed to insert the Source diskette, choose OK, since you already did this at step 2. The Copying Disk box appears, and the copy process begins.

9. When instructed to insert the target disk, remove the original disk from the drive, and insert the blank disk. Then choose OK to continue. The Copying Disk box disappears when the process is complete.

Index

Symbols

(pound signs), 102
// (slashes), 102
:: (colons), 102
<< button, 8
>> button, 8
... (ellipsis), 138
3-D effects for objects, 93-94
35mm slides, 12-13

A-B

accelerator keys, 137
alignment in text boxes, 37
Apply Scheme tool, 100
Apply Style buttons, 5
Arc tool, 3, 54-55
arcs, drawing, 54-55
arrows
    adding to lines, 54
    after commands, 138
audience handouts, 118-120
    printing, 130-132

Back button, 8
background items, 101-105
backups, Windows original
    diskettes, 141-142
Body object, 26-28
Bullet button, 44
bulleted lists, 27-31
bullets, 44-46

C

cells, editing, 71-72
Chart window, 80
check boxes, 139
circles, drawing, 57
clearing Datasheet cells, 71-72
clicking, 136
clip art, 61-64
Clip Art libraries, opening, 61-62
closing presentations, 16-17
colons (::), 102
color schemes, 96-100
colors
    graphs, 78-79
    pictures, 66-67
    text, 50-51
columns
    Datasheet, 72-74
    tabbed, 40-42
command buttons, 140
commands
    Arrange Group, 95
    Arrange Regroup, 95
    Arrange Ungroup, 95
    Chart Add Legend, 79-80
    Chart Delete Legend, 80
    Disk Copy Disk (Windows File
        Manager), 141-142
    Edit Apply Scheme, 100
    Edit Clear, 86
    Edit Copy, 36, 85
    Edit Cut, 36, 84
    Edit Duplicate, 115

D

E

F-G

H-J

K